SUPER CHARACTER DESIGN & POSES

Vol.1 HERO

by

YOU KUSANO

SUPER CHARACTER / DESIGN & POSES
Vol.1 HERO

by You Kusano©

First original bilingual edition was published in 2001
by MPC Publishing Co., Ltd.
1-10-1, Uchi-kanda, Chiyoda-ku Tokyo 101-0047, Japan
URL : http://www.mpc-world.co.jp/

Author : You Kusano
Editing : Jun Itoh
DTP : Tsukuru Morita, Jun Itoh, Massan
Translasiton : Tsukuru Morita, Suzi Yamaguchi, Excite-kun

Distributor
Japan Publications Trading Co., Ltd.
1-2-1 Sarugaku-cho, Chiyoda-ku, Tokyo 101-0064, Japan
E-mail : jpt@jptco.co.jp
URL : http://www.jptco.co.jp/

First Printing : August 2003

ISBN4-88996-121-6
Printed in Japan

ABOUT THIS BOOK

The main theme of this book is how to draw tough and hard-boiled characters and thier expressions, costumes, and arms. The collection of poses might be a reference guide for drawing your original work.

WORKS

This chapter shows the process for creating a new character. Based on a theme, this section focusses on the rough sketch until the finish. I have tried to summerize it so it is easily understood. I have included a variation of heroes from different genres and tried to recreate them as "hard" characters.

BODY

This chapter explains the basic stages of how to create a character. It includes how to draw the smart body indespensable to "super" characters. I have simply and effectively compared different variations of eyes and nose, and included paints regarding face and hair.

PEN&TECHNIQUE

Although this chapter seems small, we have edited it to include the necessary fundamental techniques which can be obtained easily with minimum effort.

POSES

This chapter as the name suggests, is a collection of poses. I think what makes this book attractive is the unification of technique and poses. This includes poses which are usually difficult to draw and about 200 commmonly drawn poses. As I am an illustrator, when I compiled this collection of poses I kept in mind "wouldn't it be great to have a collection of poses like this". Where possible, the characters that appear in this collection do not wear clothes. I have drawn them with a T-shirt or tank top so you can easily understand the body motion and form. You can add clothing and complete your own characters.

CONTENTS

Super Character's

WORKS

■WORKS■

HALF BREED

A halfbreed of god and satan.
He is a proud but lonely hero.
With the image of a man carrying a misfortune destiny, create a hard and wild character.

1 one Atmosphere like the son of the devil has occurred as an image.

2 two Make his body slim and sexy but keep the muscular quality.

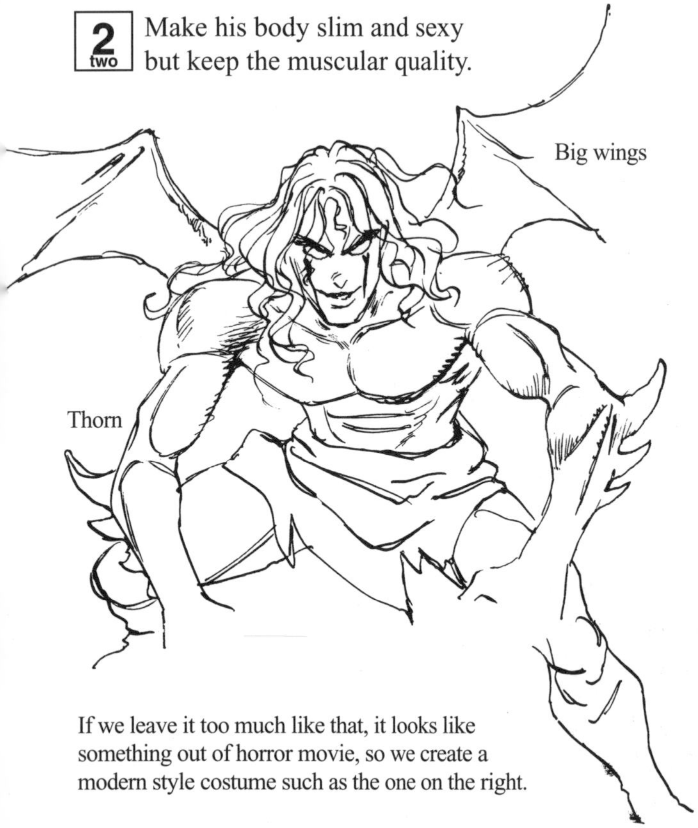

3 three Almost complete

HALF BREED

WORKS

SHADOW

The solitary hero with a dark past.
An ally of the justice who has the capability to disguise himself and manipulates a whip.
His name is "shadow".

1 one It is a character like the so-called Batman or Superman. Once he is transformed into a character, I want his whole body in an armor like costume. I always start with the face when create a character

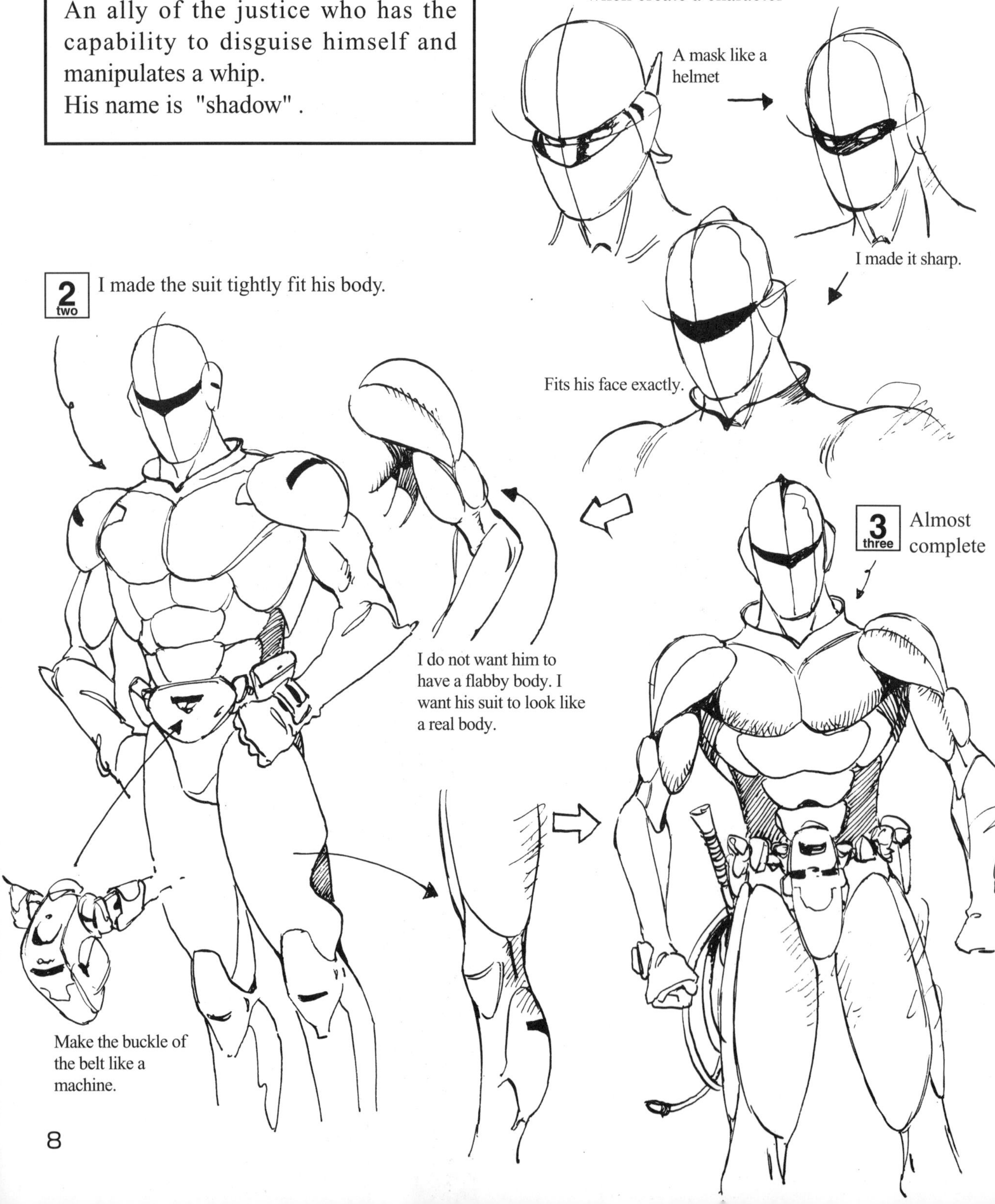

SHADOW

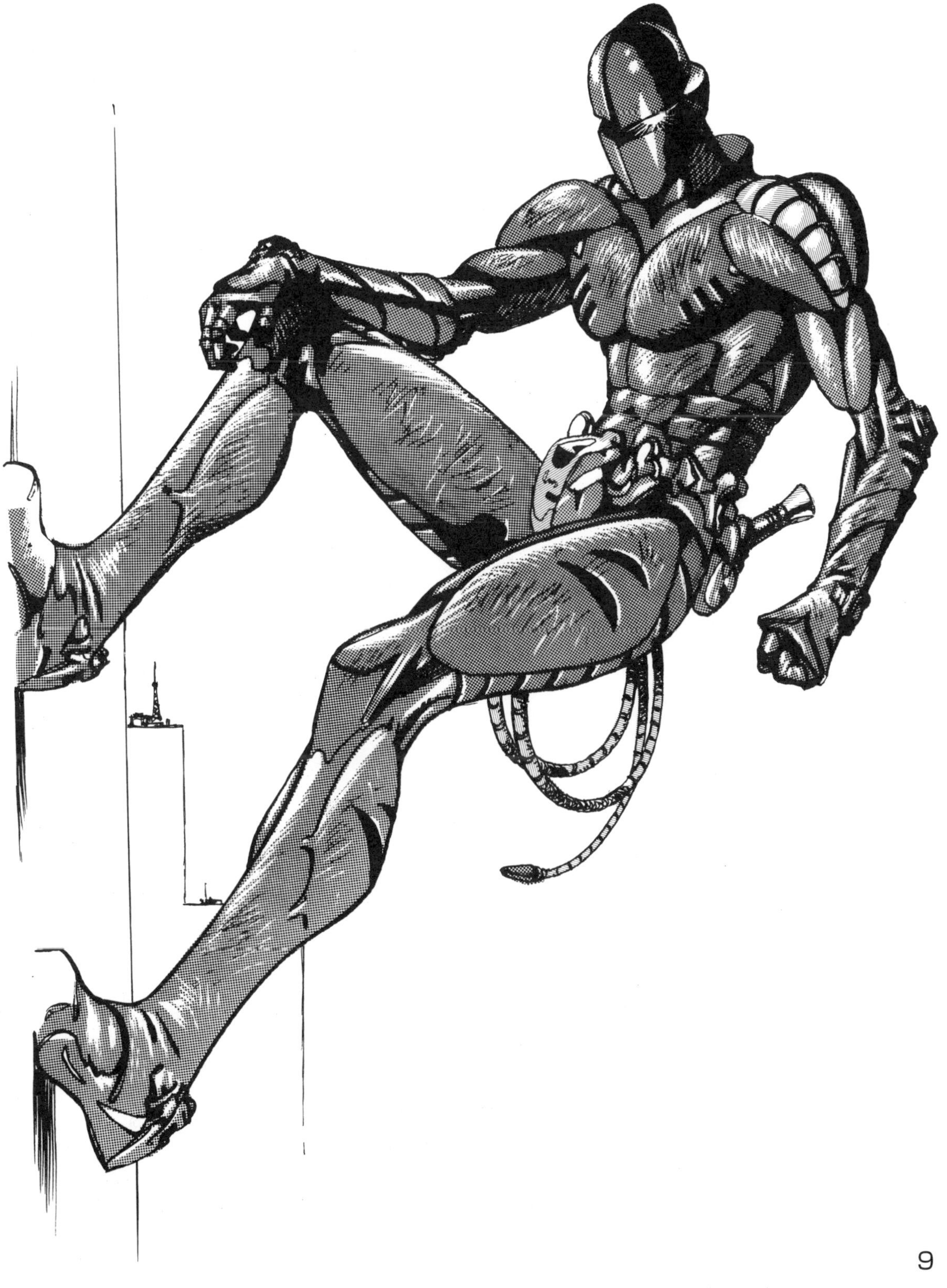

■WORKS■

METALIC WOMAN

Let's create a sexy heroine who has full-metalic body.

1 one Think of an image for her face and do a rough sketch.

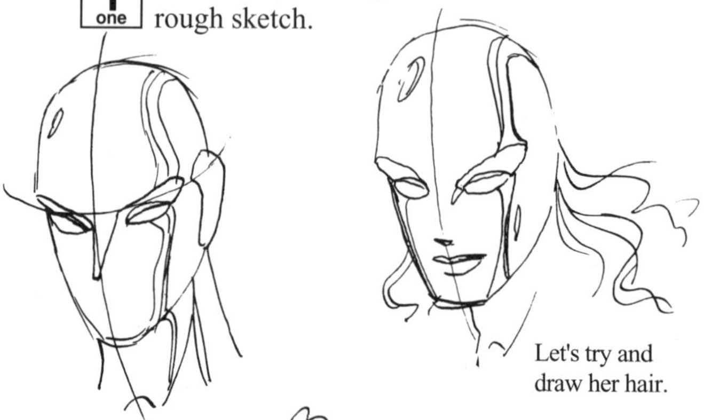

Let's try and draw her hair.

2 two The image of a face is done. I will make the skin metallic and will create a sexy costume.

I thought about an armor but it seemed dowdy.

3 three Almost complete

Instead of attaching an armor,
we made her body brawny.

We made her image dressy by adding gloves and a simple swimming suit.

METALIC WOMAN

PLATINA LADY

■WORKS■

HORROR HERO

A young man has been made the guinea pig of DNA research by an evil organization.
However, experiment failed and he is transmitted into an muscular monster.
Give me back! He raises a sad cry and continues a solitary fight against an evil organization.

1 one Since the image is a "muscular monster", I decided to make it like a specimen of the human body.

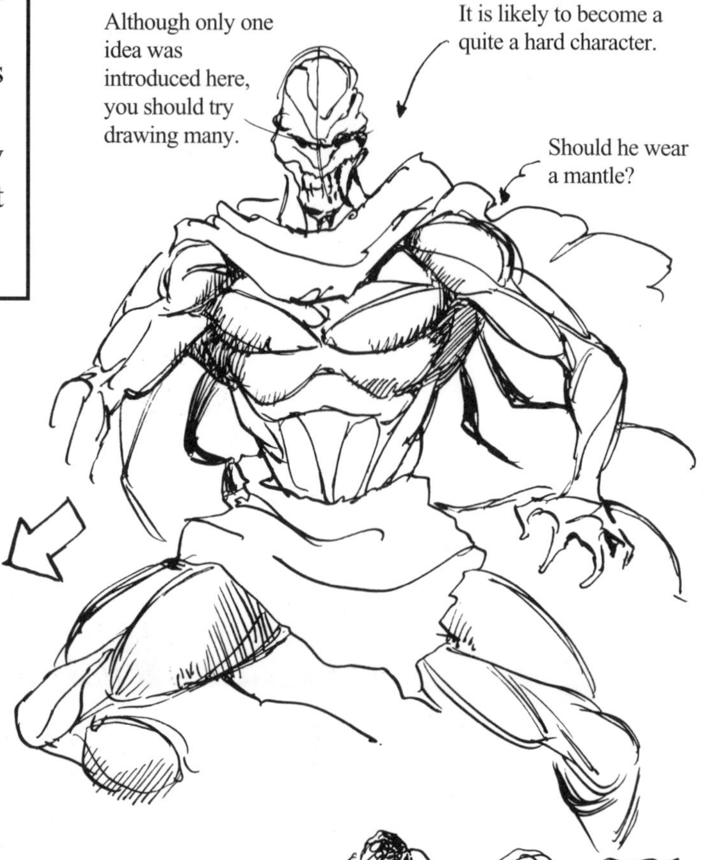

2 two Muscles are added after the image of the skull.

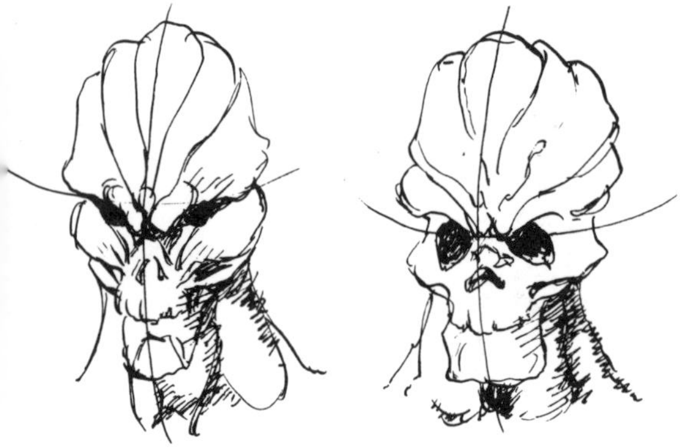

We added the bondage mask to coordinate with his clothes.
The bondage is a necessary, which is also effective in producing pity.

3 three Modulate with shading for completion.

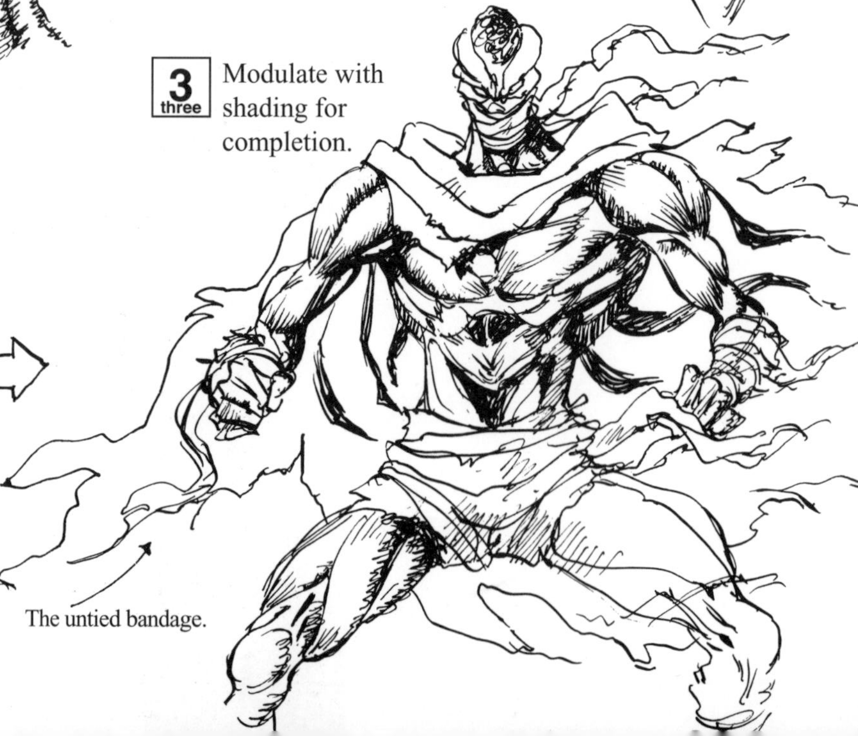

HORROR HERO

THE MUSCLE

Give me back!

■WORKS■

FUTURE COMMANDO

This hero is a mischievous nonconformist.
Although he is skillful, he may disregard commands and clash with his superiors.
He protects justice.

1 one First, I take into consider the hero's character. I think he is a man with a tough but bright character.

2 two I decided he has a Mohawk! This unexpected nature suits the theme.

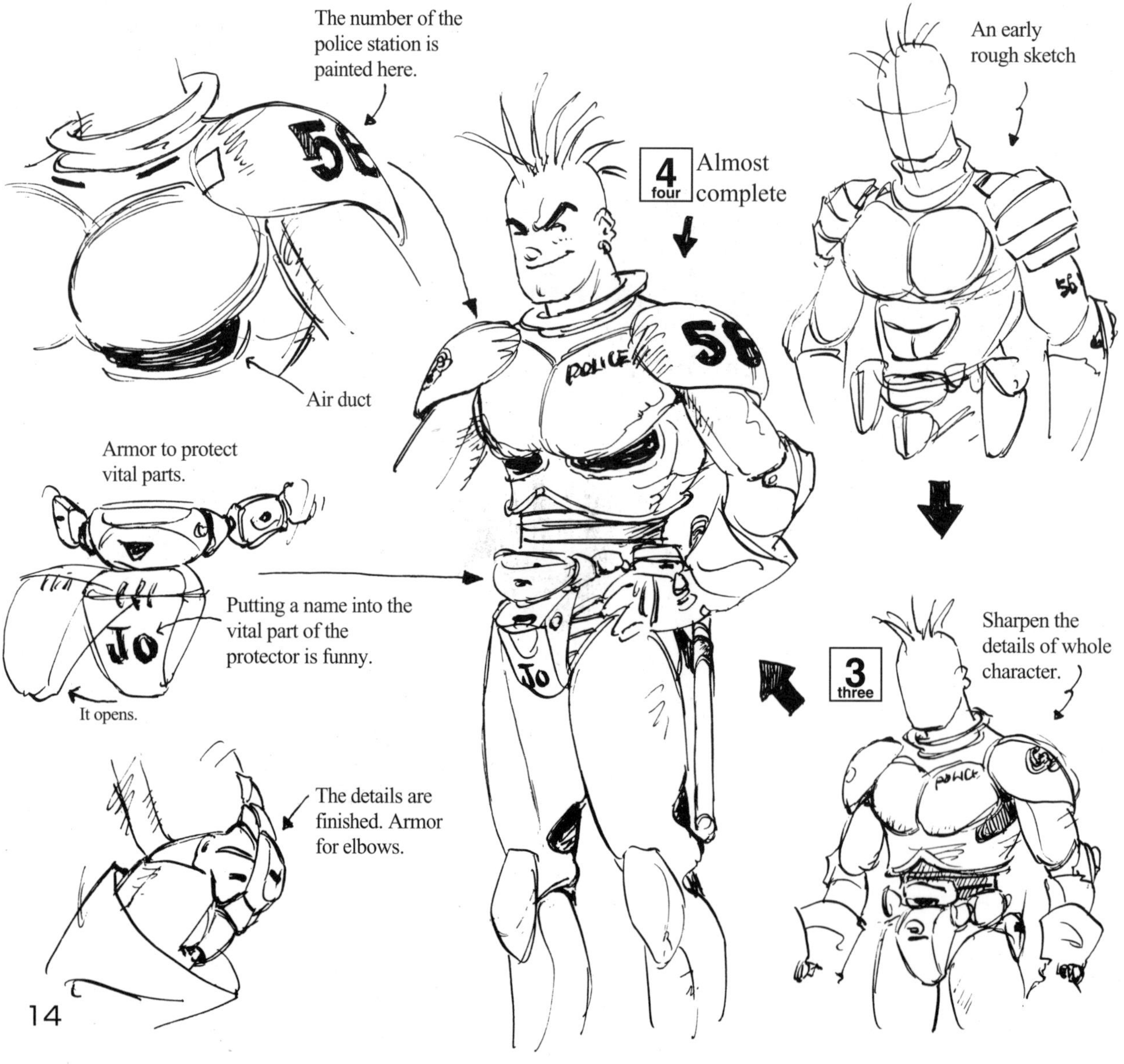

FUTURE COMMANDO

MOHAWK COP

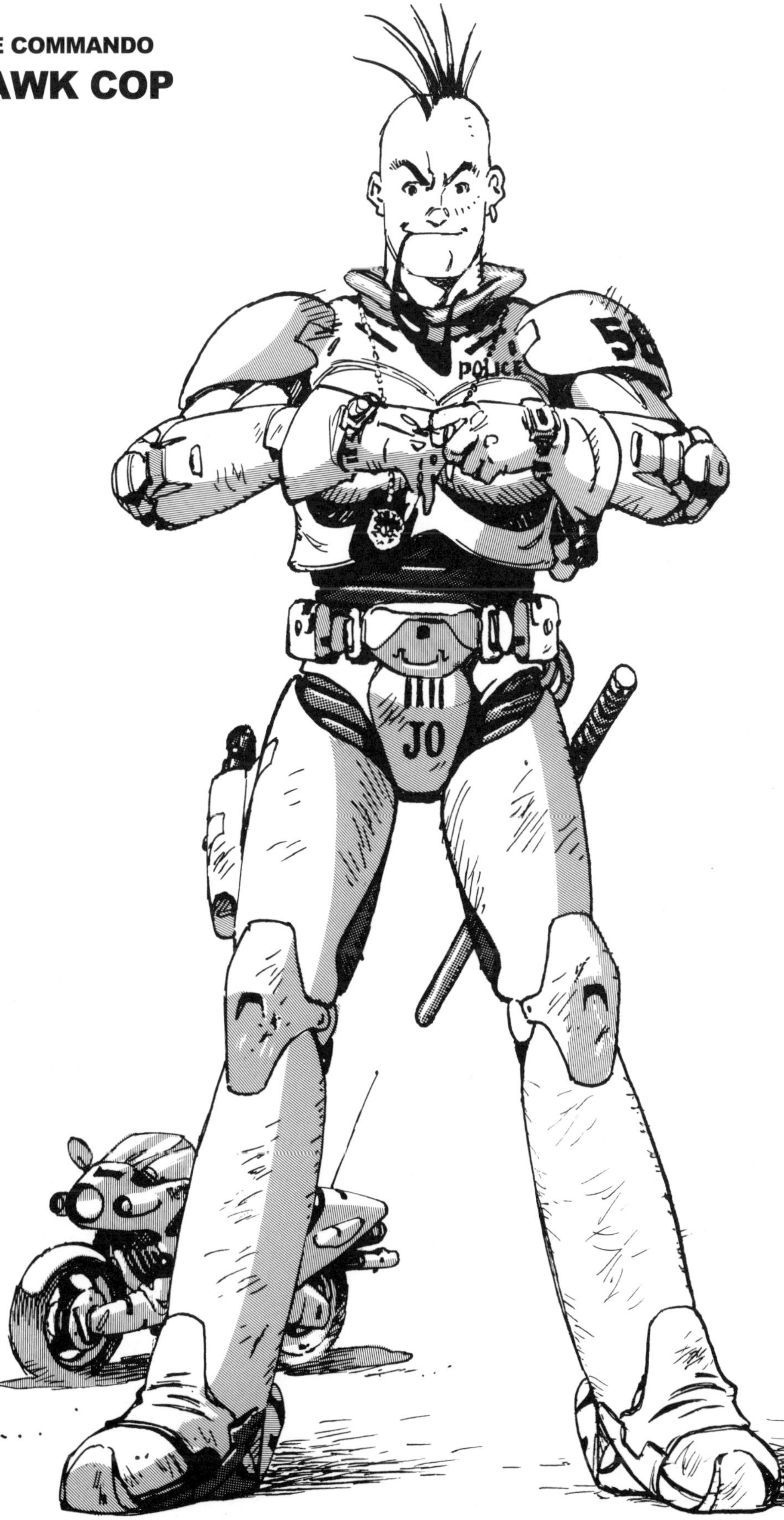

■WORKS■

HAMIDASHI COP

He is a nonconformist detective who finds his soul in Bushido and Sumo.
Topknot and Japanese swords etc are keywords that characterize him.
He is not a classy man, he is more like a downtown bully.

1 one Although we begin with the face again this time, it is easy to do since we are attaching a topknot (chommage).

Rather, it should be like samurai hair.

It looks much more realistic if moved to the right. We make him a little fatter, black and give him a topknot. He looks like a black sumo wrestler. Looks great!

2 two The image has appeared clearly by drawing the face. He is not slim, the body was fattened to look more like a sumo wrestler.

Here he is too fat and looks more like a superhero so I will change it a little.

3 three Almost complete

We made him more stern here so he wouldn't look like a super hero like in the left picture.

Added a karate belt.

HAMIDASHI COP

HARD SOUL

I will defend the 11th section!

■WORKS■

WOMAN COP

This hero is a woman.
A specialist in perverted crimes, she has a dark past.
She is an excellent detective.

1 one This time also we start with the face. Since it is quite a hard female detective's image, short hair is also considered. Sunglasses are indispensable.

This was too intelligent.

Although she has long hair, we can improve it by pulling it up in a ponytail. She is still feminine.

It was decided that she would have long hair.

2 two I will emphasize her hard image with a body like a body builder.

Her clothes are simple, jeans and tank top to highlight her body line.

Scars were added to her body to reveal her dark past.

3 three Completion

WOMAN COP

MARIA ANGEL

■WORKS■

THE COOL KILLER

The kind of action hero who you see often.
A so-called cool and fashionable character.
He has long hair, sunglasses, leather trousers and a long coat.

1 one I want to create a handsome and cool character. You can make him to your own liking and style of fashion.

2 two However, you need a good sense in order to create an interesting character.

THE COOL KILLER
BULLDOG

■WORKS■

SF ADVENTURE HERO

He is one of the few survivors who bravely challenges and fights against evil.
He is a pecular man always accompained by a hawk. It's a romantic action theme.

1 one Start with his face. He has a sweet face but strong. His expression should be sad.

2 two Let's make his costume as simple as possible.

3 three Completion

SF ADVENTURE HERO

LONELY HERO

■WORKS■

SUPER HERO

He runs faster than sound and can dodge bullets.
A super hero of justice.
Super hero of all heroes.
He is the superman of the future!

1 one His face is covered with a mask. This helmet like mask is aero dynamic giving the feeling that he can run faster than sound.

After drawing several rough ideas, I decided on this mask.

2 two His body. It's better not to use a mantle since he should be aero dynamic.

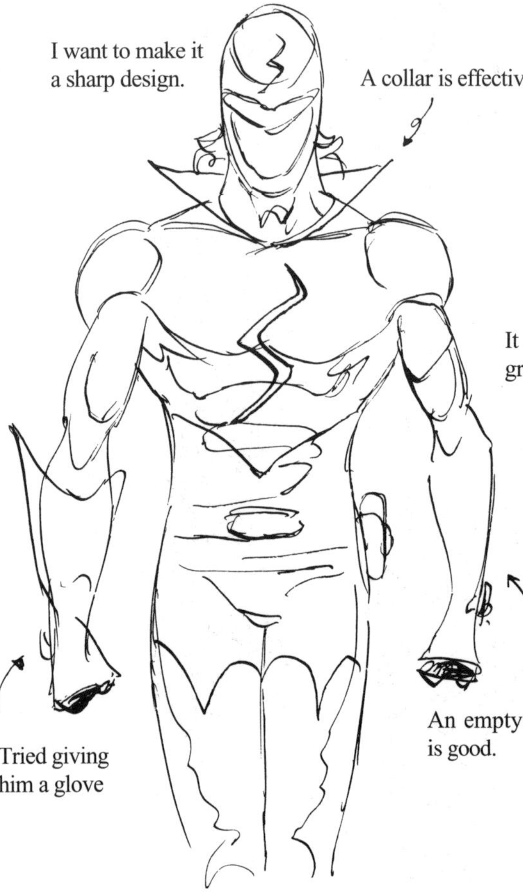

I want to make it a sharp design.

A collar is effective.

Tried giving him a glove

An empty hand is good.

It has been finished gradually.

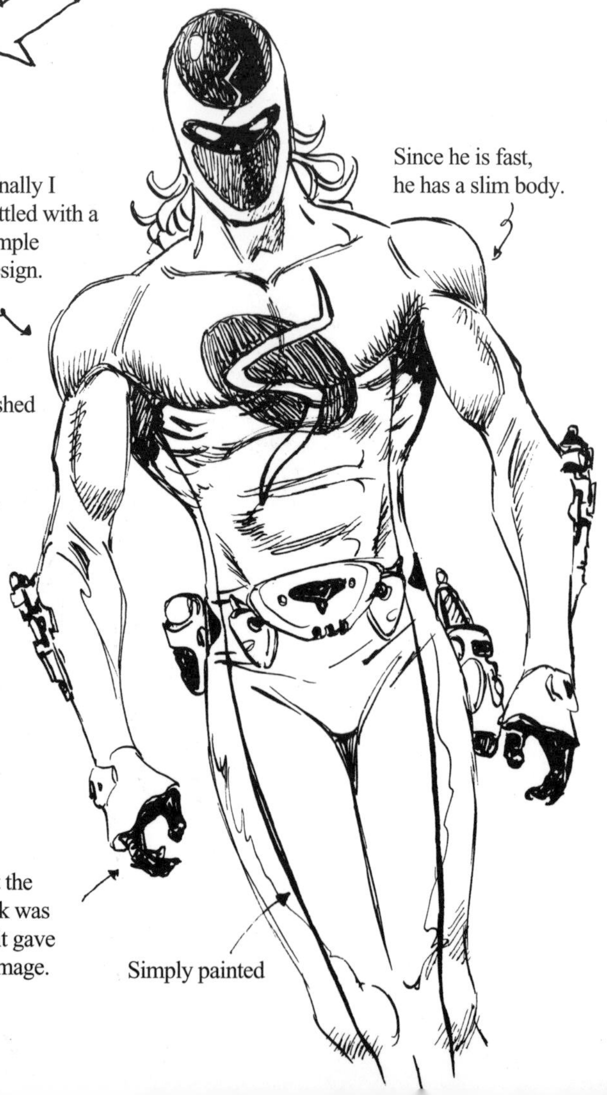

Finally I settled with a simple design.

Since he is fast, he has a slim body.

Painting just the fingers, black was effective as it gave him a hard image.

Simply painted

SUPER HERO

MAX

■WORKS■

FISH MAN

A creature which lives in the sea. Produce a monster which is a fish like alien creature.

1 one This is the image which appeared suddenly!

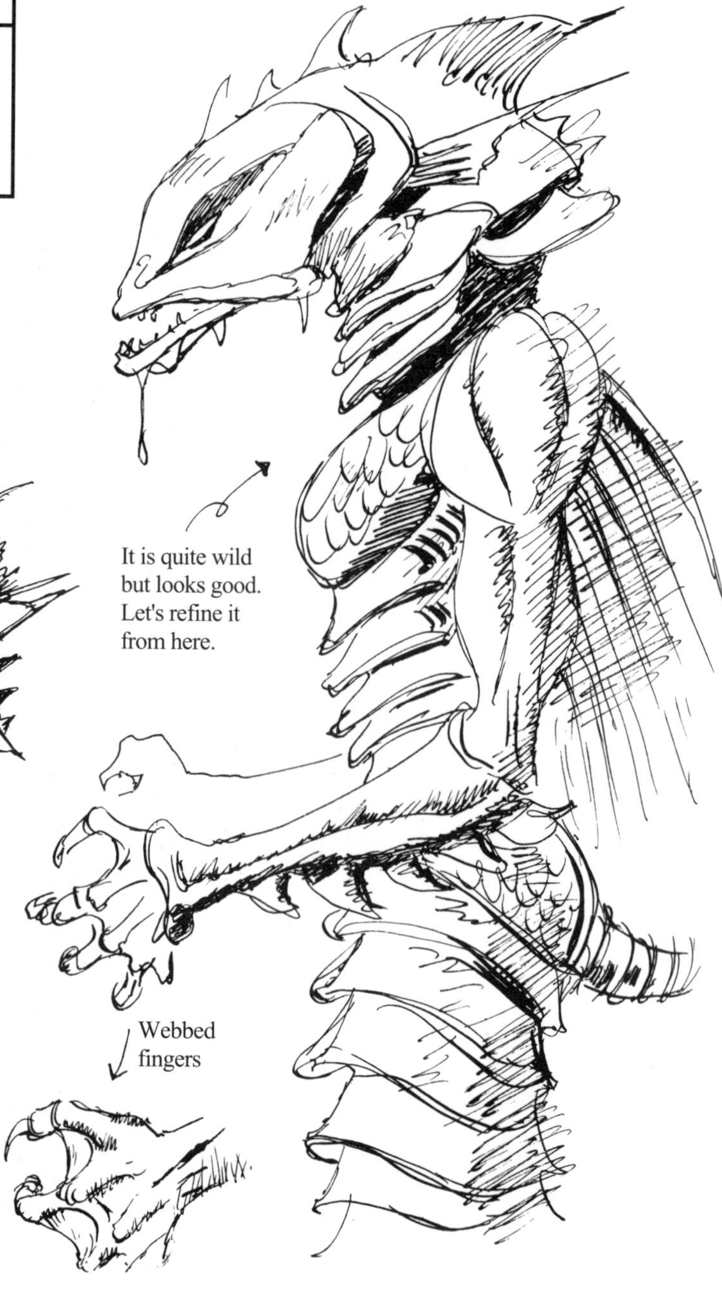

It is quite wild but looks good. Let's refine it from here.

Webbed fingers

2 two I will consider other variations.

I imagined swordfish sharpened the tip of his nose. It is not bad.

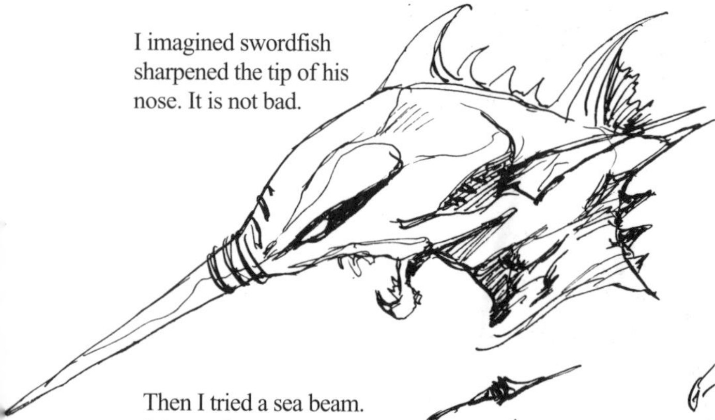

Then I tried a sea beam. It is good.

I attached hair and drew it from the front. It is quite good.

●POINT

Although the motif was a living sea creature, I decided to use the head of a fish to make it this time. From the initial stages I had imagined a salmon with a sharp mouth.

FISH MAN

Super Character's

BODY

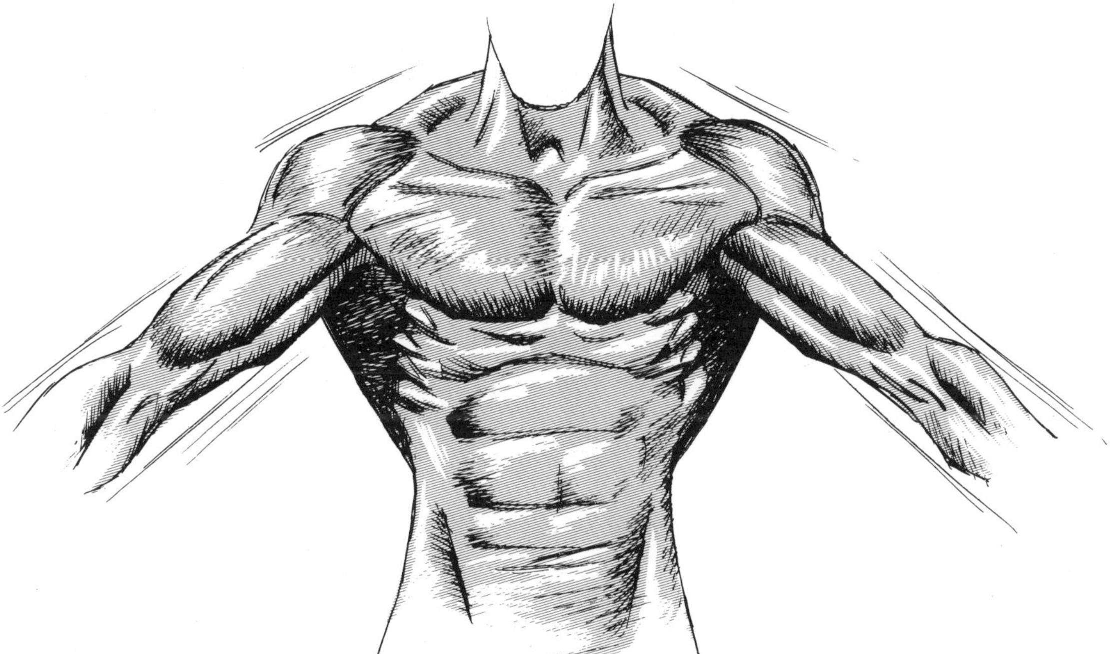

■BODY■

SUPER BODY

A super character needs a hard and tough body.

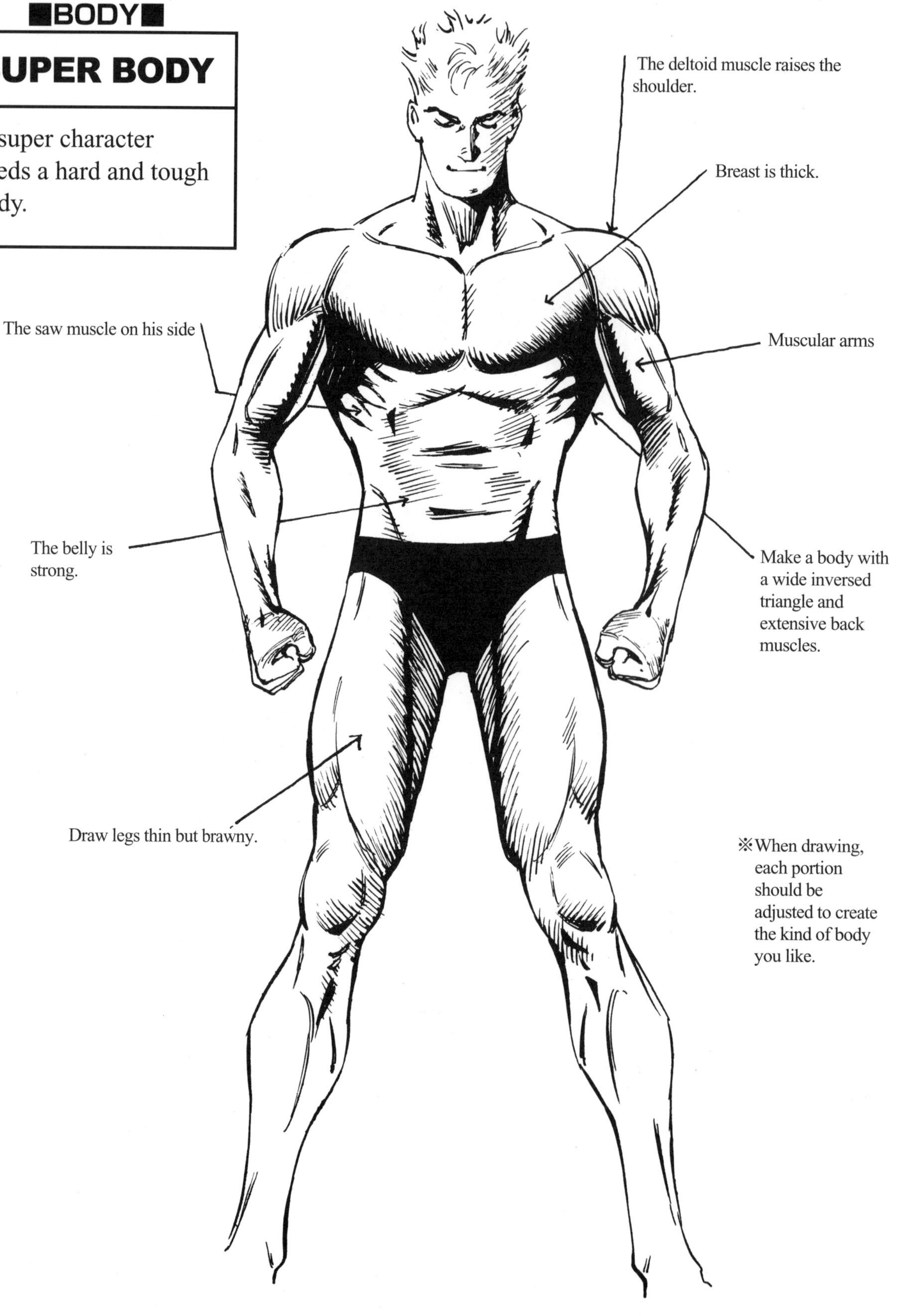

※When drawing, each portion should be adjusted to create the kind of body you like.

■BODY■

SIDE

The body seen from the side

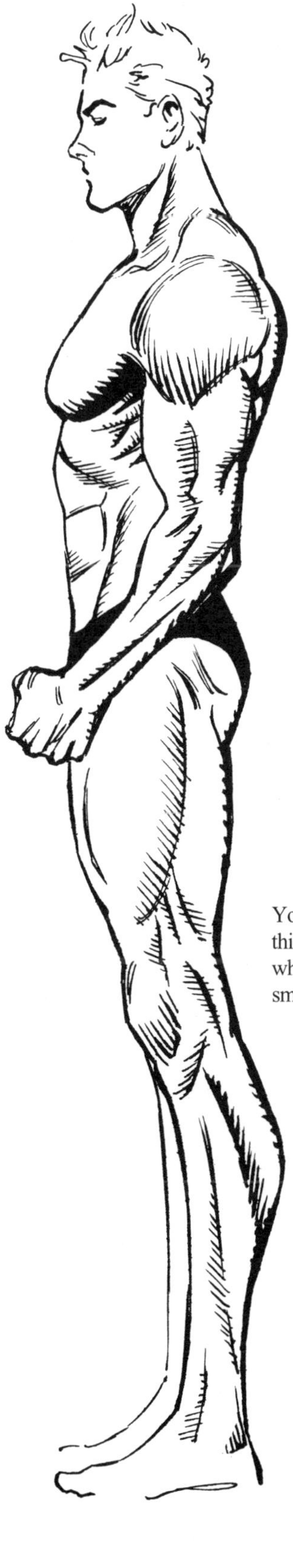

Emphasize the thickness and hardness of the breast.

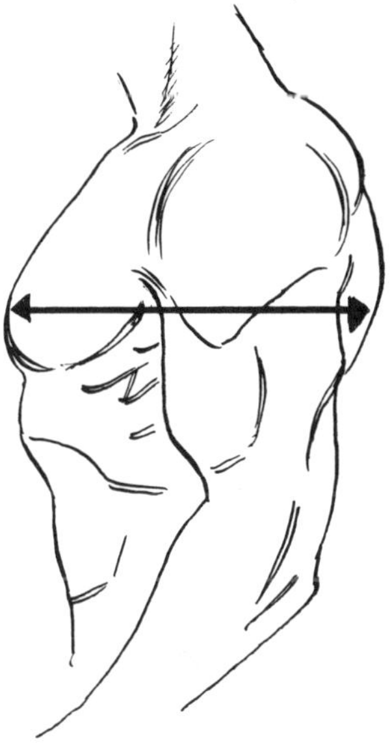

The body becomes like an arch while standing ordinarily.

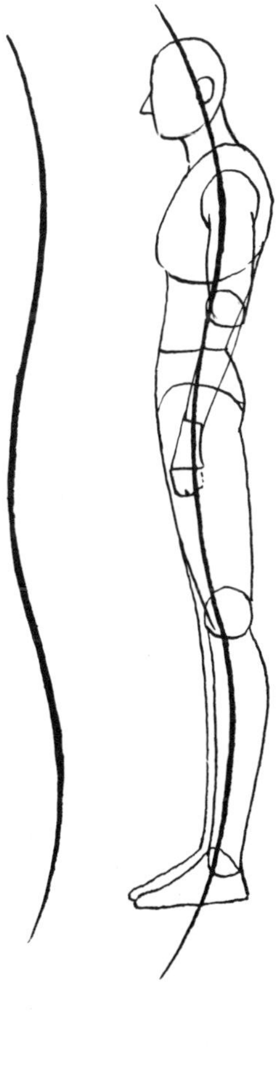

You can emphasize the thickness of the legs while keeping them smart.

■BODY■

BACK

The body seen from the back

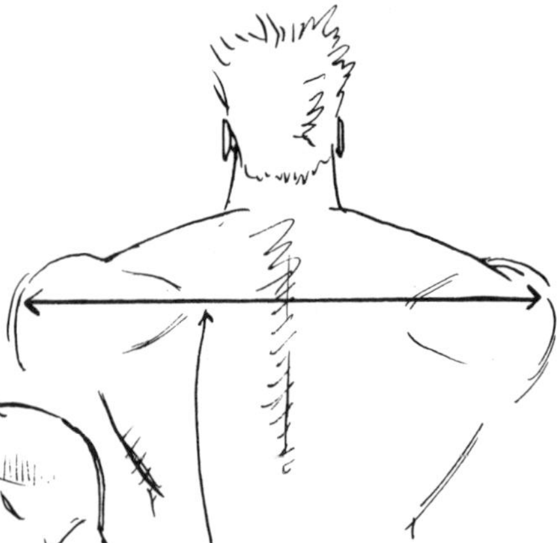

The larger you make the breadth of his sholders, the bigger and stronger he becomes.

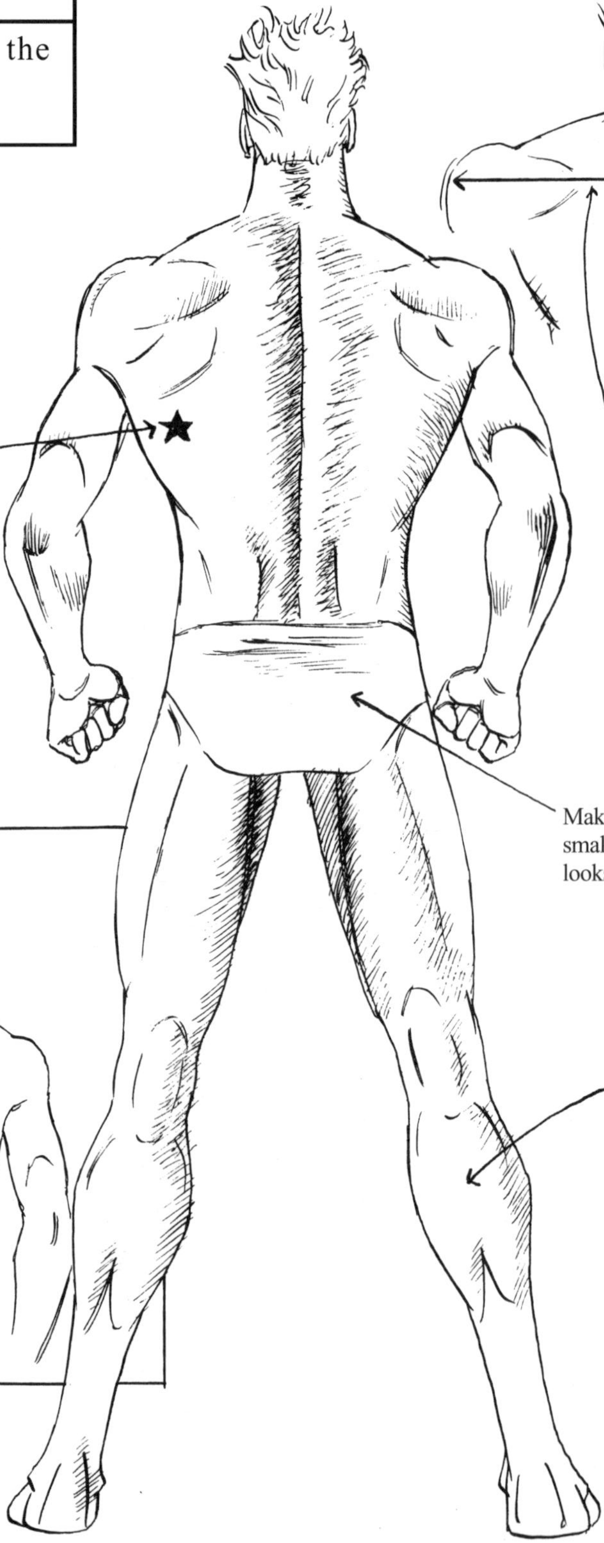

Make a body with an inversed triangle shaped back with a brawny latissimus dorsi muscle.

Make his hip slightly smaller so he still looks smart.

Soleus muscle should be thick and brawny.

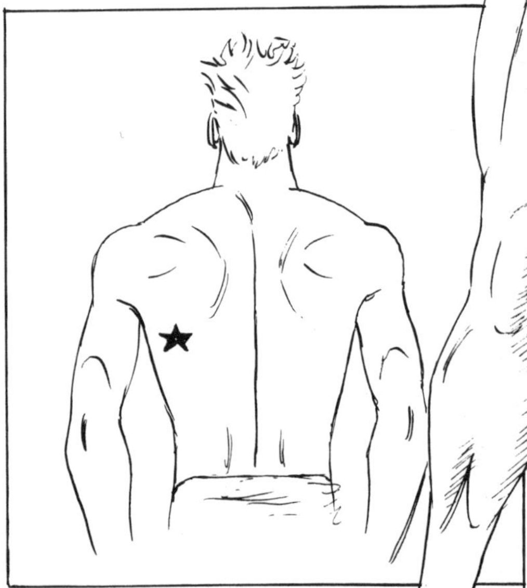

A narrow latissimus dorsi muscle

BODIES

I have compared the different bodies and I want you to notice the difference in power.

A little over exaggeration is good.
So study different styles and create your favorite bodies.

An ordinary physique

This is quite a hard build.
He is tall and each part of his body is big.
I often use this build.

This is an even bigger build.
He has a build like a body builder.

UNDERSTANDING BODY

You should know the motion of the muscle of the upper body. You can realistically draw a body if you know how the breast and shoulder muscle move when an arm is moved up or down.

●The motion of muscle●

I want you to be careful of the movement of the breast muscle when the arm is extended up (left) and horizontally(right).

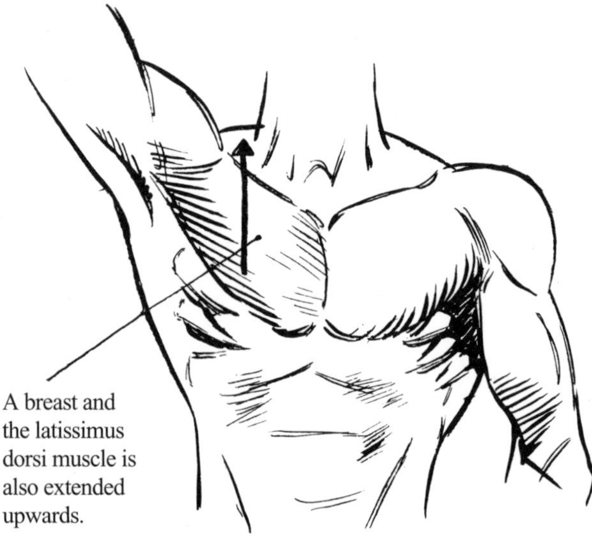

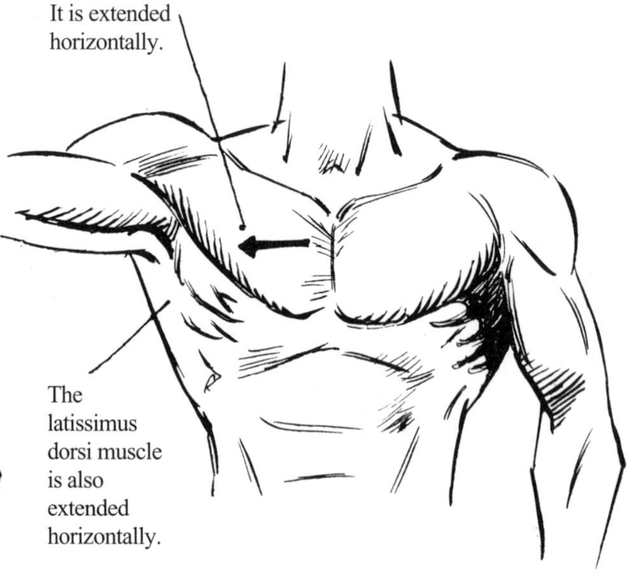

BREAST

●The motion of muscle●

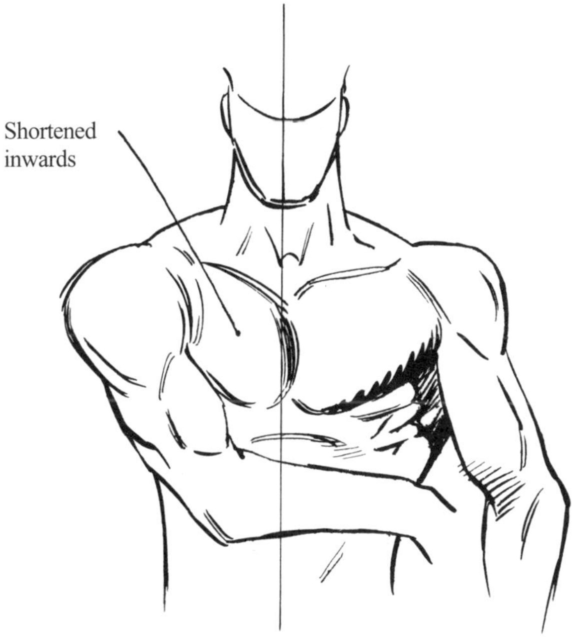

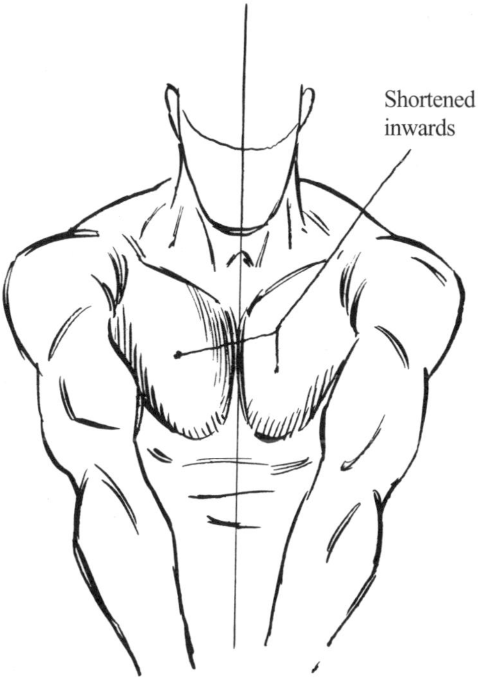

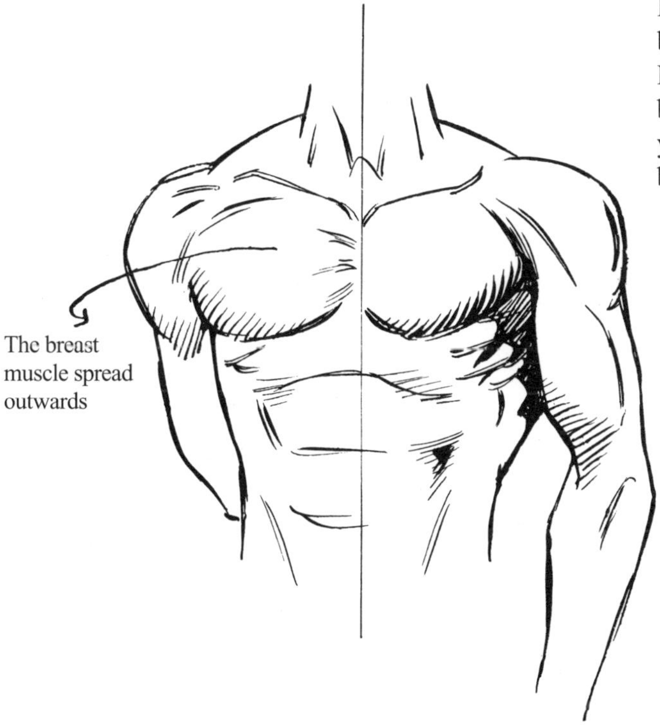

Place a mirror on your desk, look at your own body and how it moves.
Muscle movement is the same in everyone's body, so imagine you have lots of muscle on your own body and let's try and draw a brawny body.

■BODY■

BREAST

●The motion of muscle●

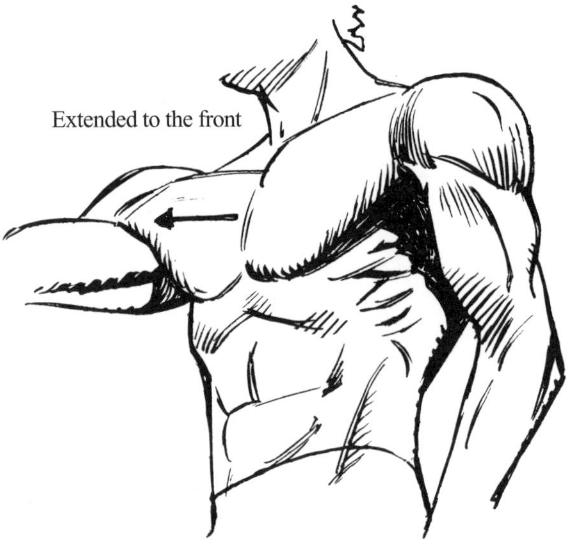

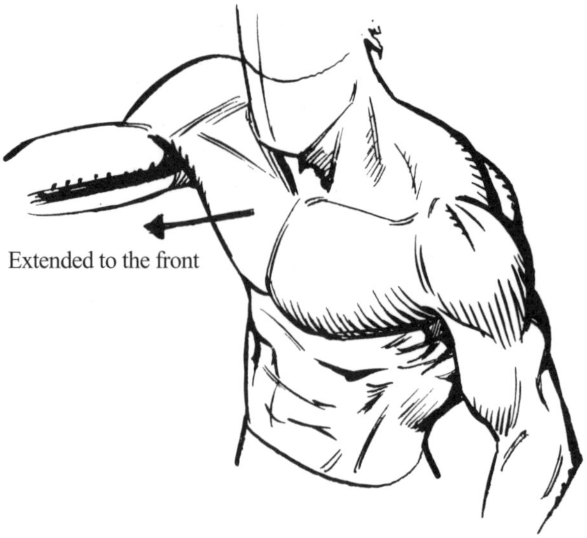

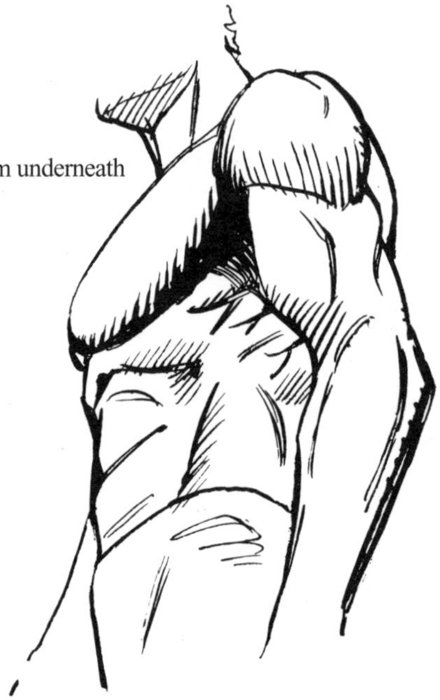

LEG

First, let's understand the structure of legs. Legs are thin when seen from the front and broad when seen from the side. From the side legs should be drawn slightly curved.

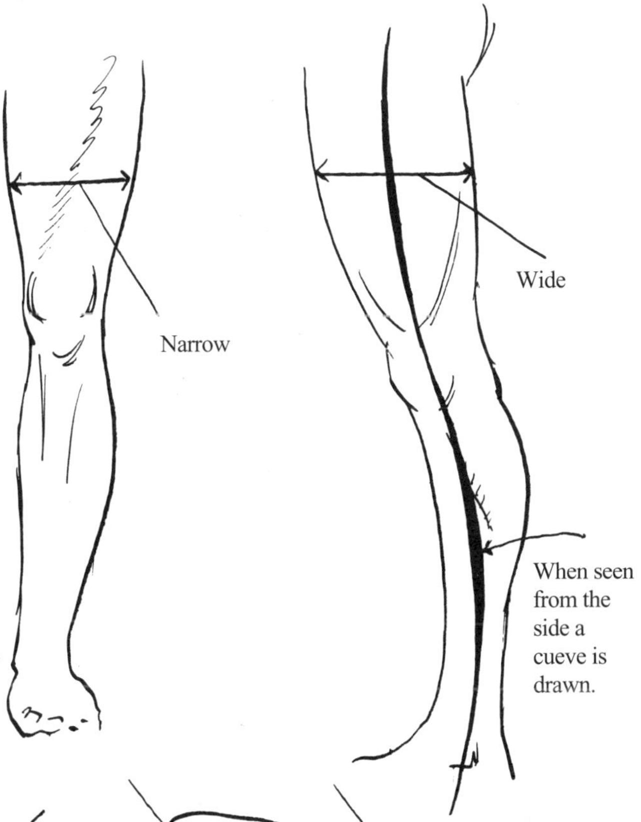

●The structure of legs●

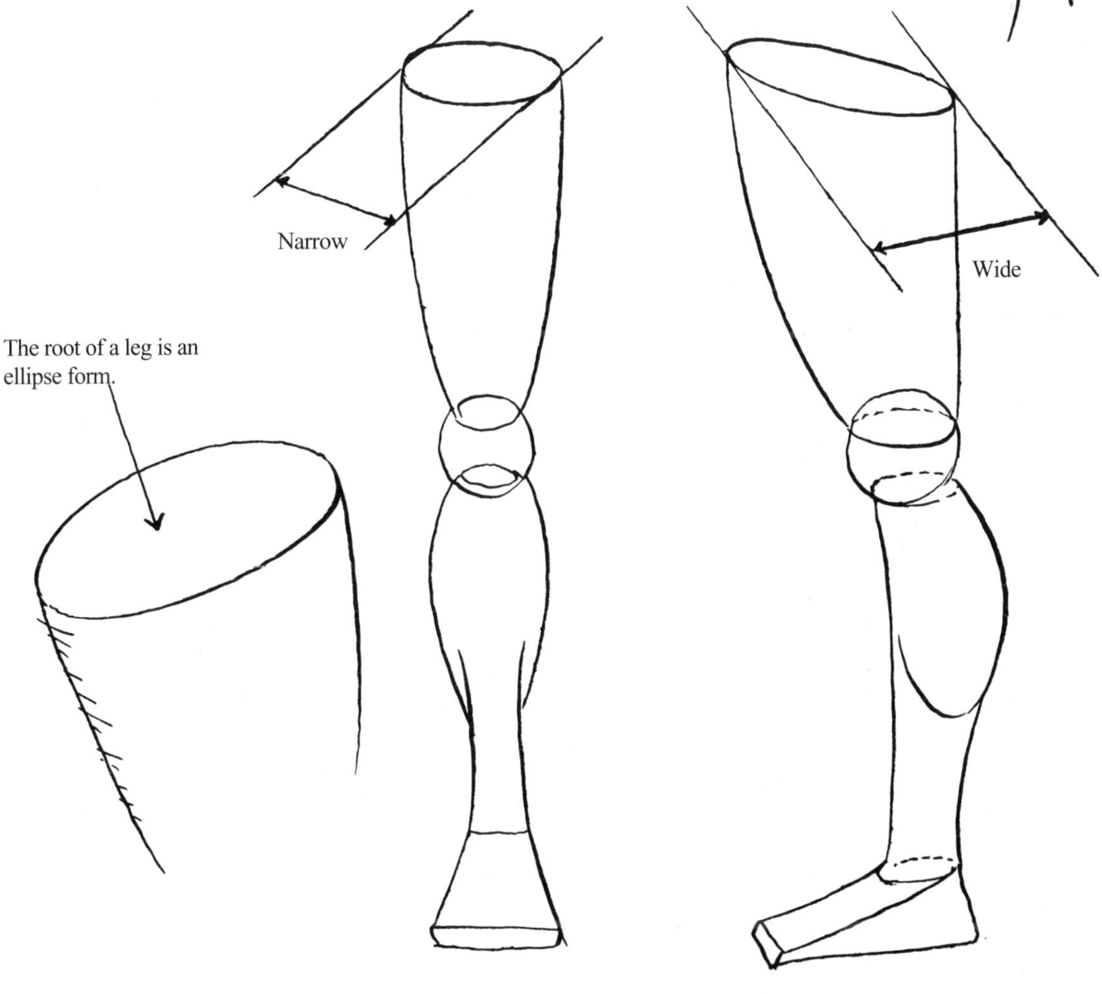

LEG

●The motion of muscle●

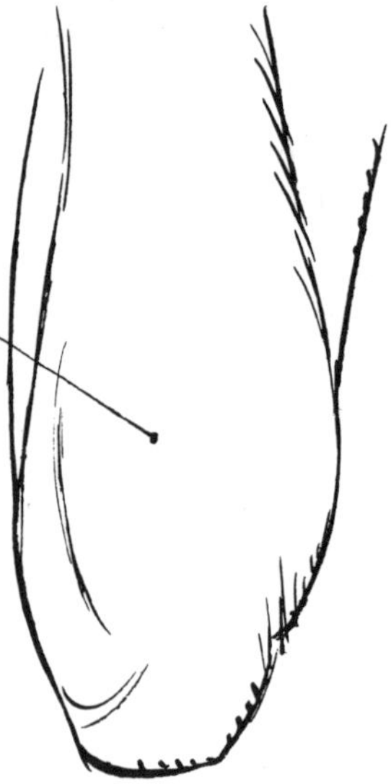

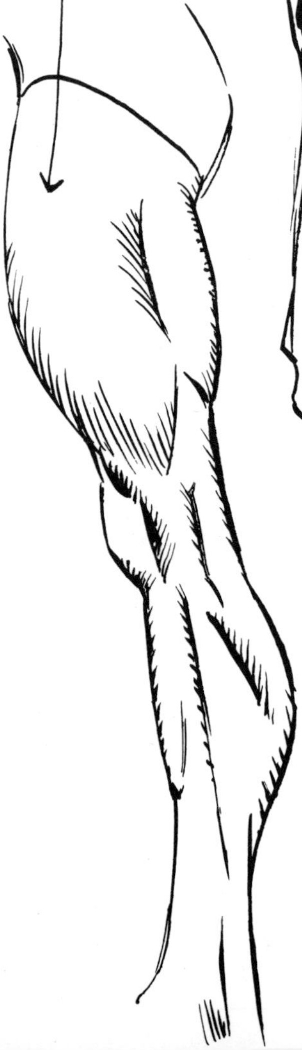

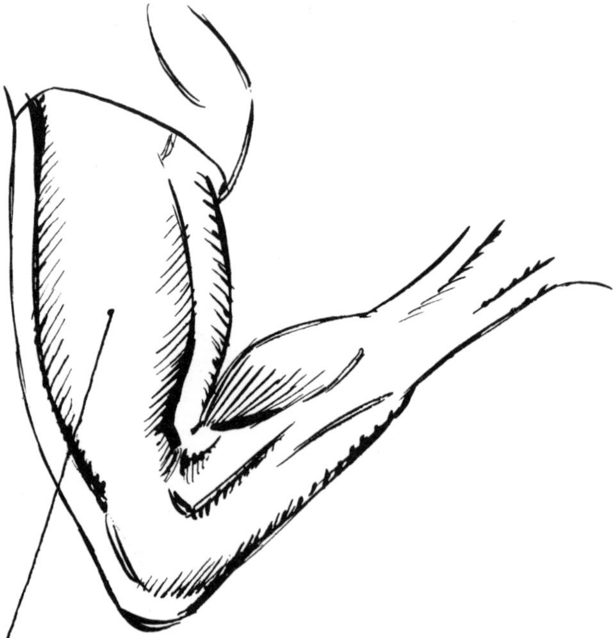

ARM

First, we should understand the structure of the whole arm. An arm is the same as a leg, when seen from the front, it is thin, and it is broad when seen from the side.

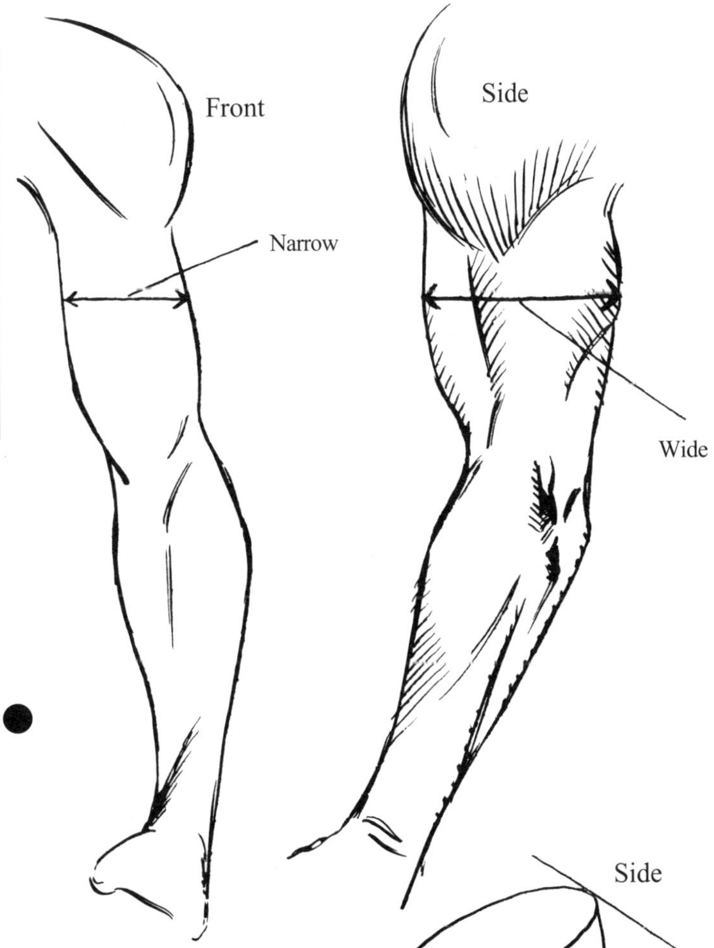

●The structure of arms●

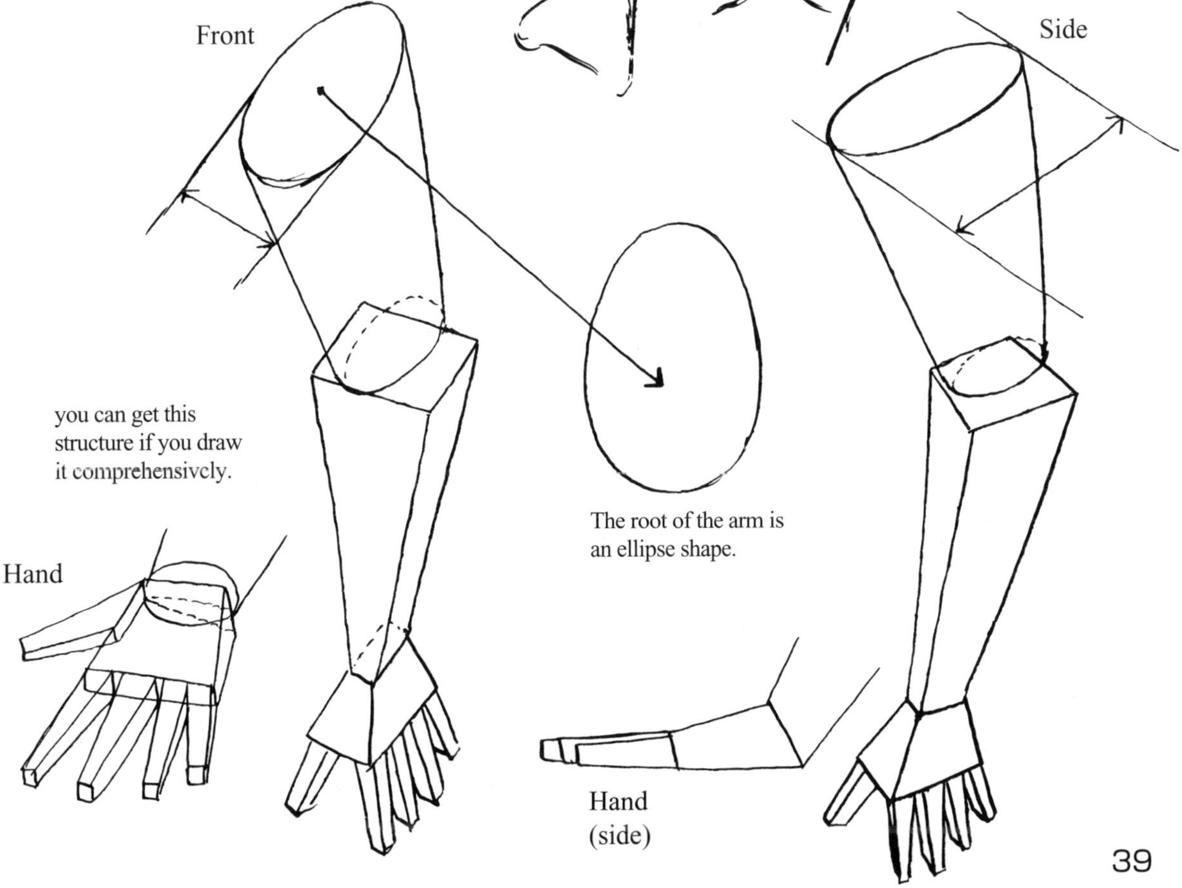

ARM

●The motion of muscle●

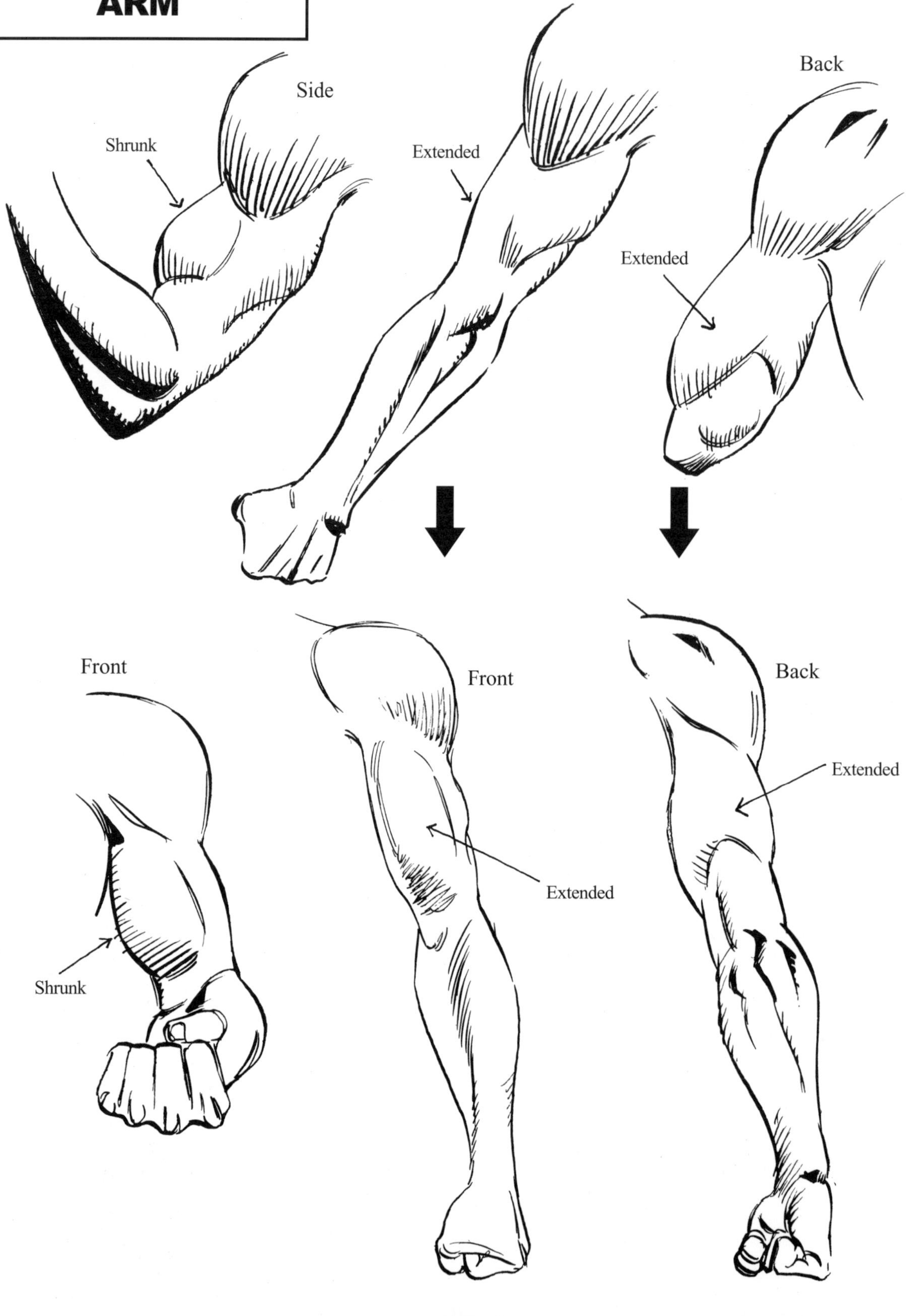

■BODY■

HAND

Look in the mirror and draw your own hand.

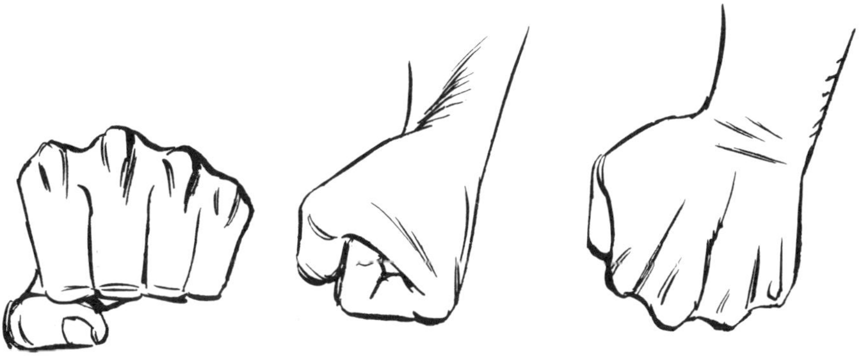

When a palm is drawn linearly, it is cool.

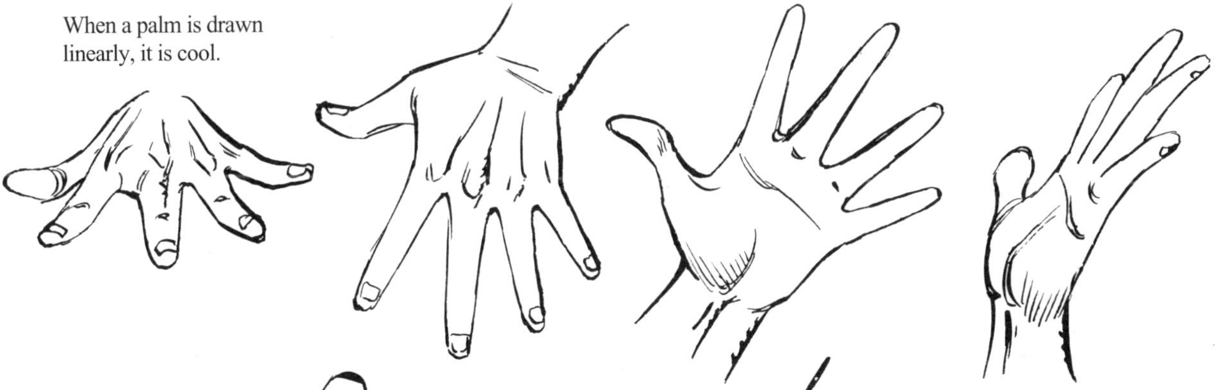

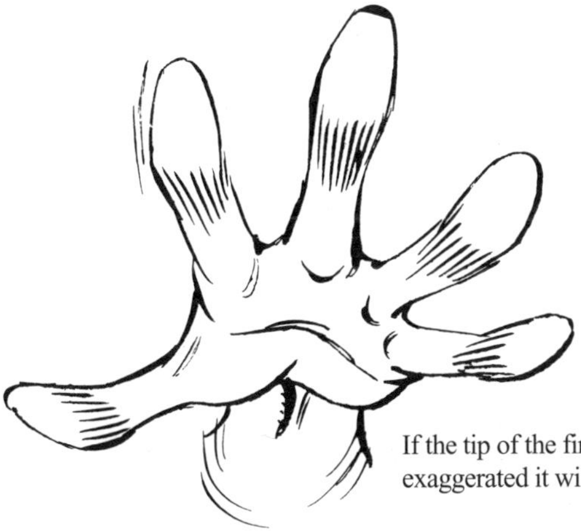

If the tip of the finger is exaggerated it will show the force.

●POINT

When you bring your finger tips close to your eyes as seen in the illustration on the right, you can see the power of finger tips. At this time, close one eye and look with the other.

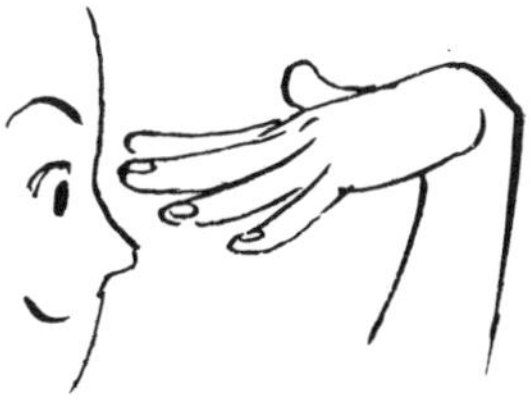

Showing the power of the finger tip

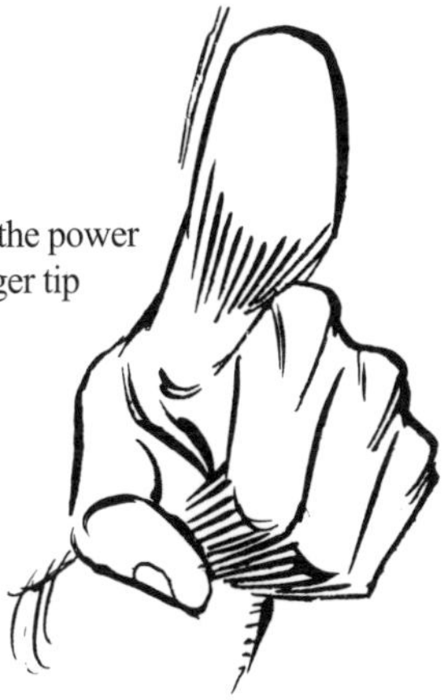

This is how I learned to draw the body.

When I was young, and studying drawing very hard, I wondered what the fastest way to become good at drawing would be.
At first, I would buy prowrestling books and magazines and try to copy it but then I started tracing over the pictures.
I thought that by tracing it repeatedly my hand would memorize it.
I would trace over it again and again until the book become tattered.

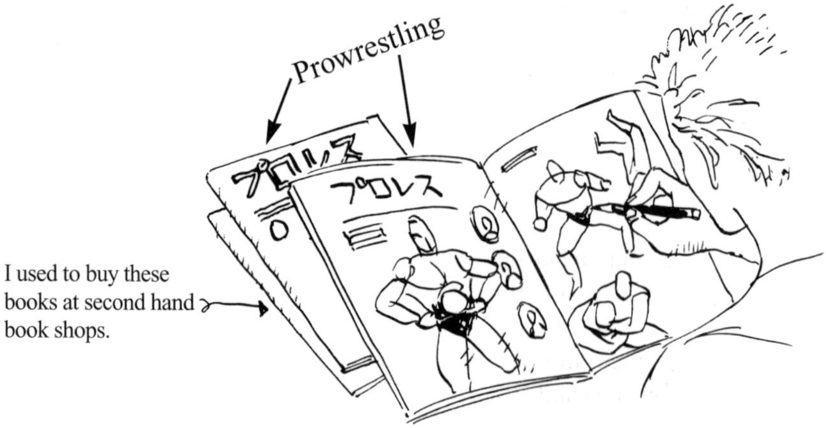

Super Character's

FACE

■FACE■

UNDERSTANDING FACE

Try to understand the foundations of the face. Althogh there are many books about facial expressions you still have to understand the fundamentals.

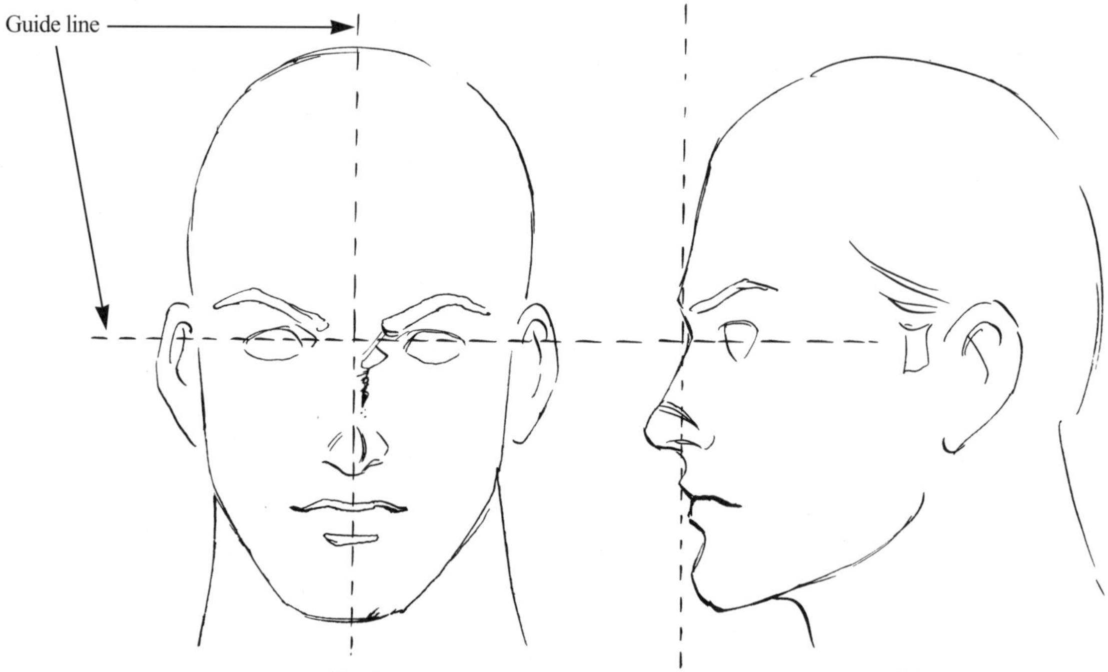

Front

Side

The jaw has come out.

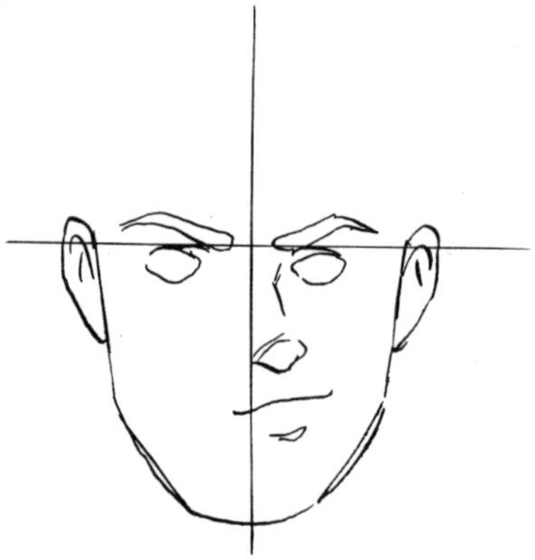

The face is bent.

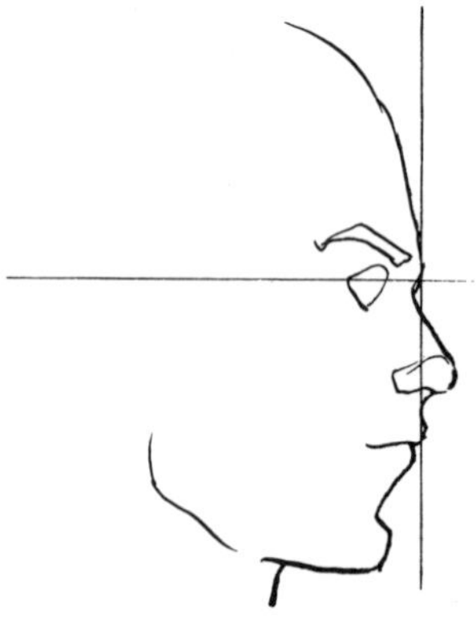

The jaw is dented.

■FACE■

EYE

●The position of eyes●

Study how a face changes according to the position and kind of eyes, as shown in the upper figure. I want you to think of an individualistic face.

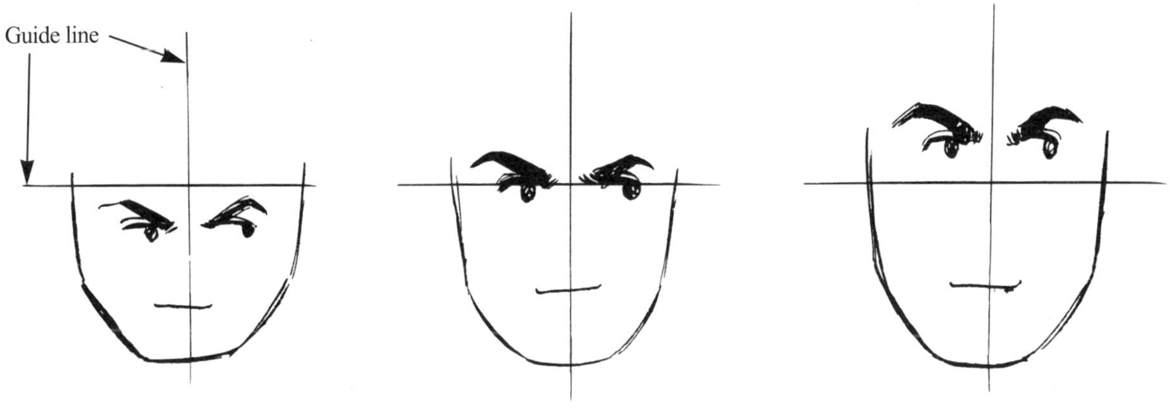

●The variation of eyes●

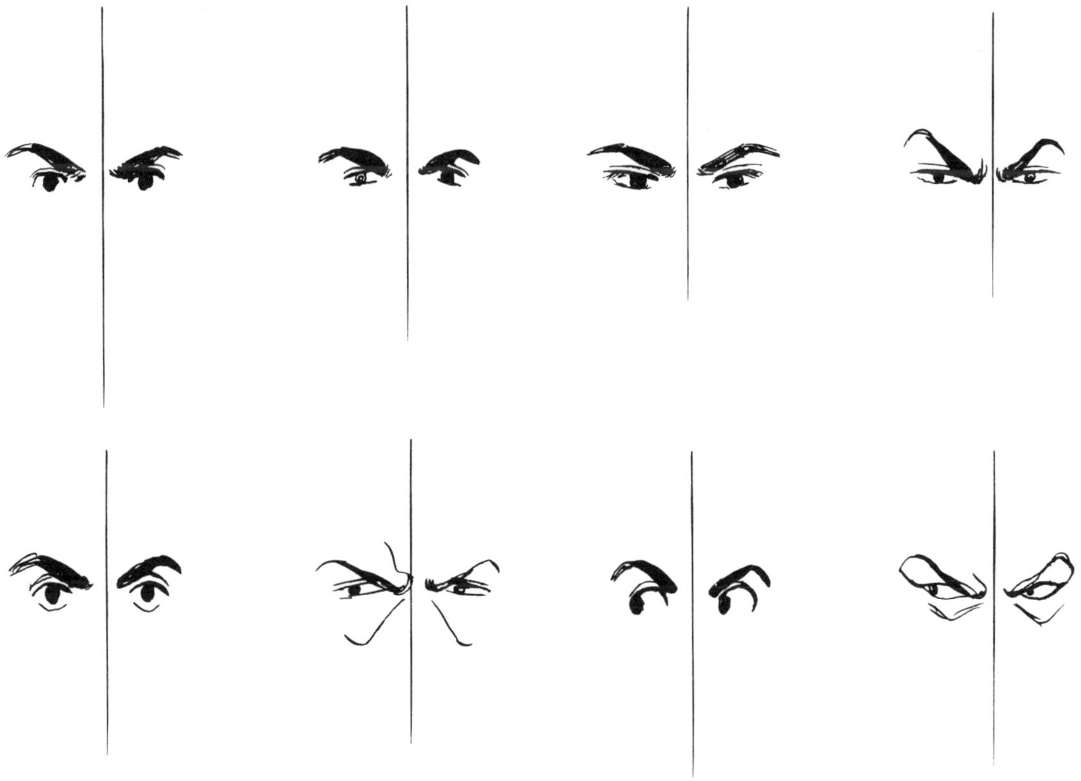

■FACE■

NOSE

As shown in the right figure, the expression of a face changes with the position and kind of nose. You should be careful to make sure that the nose on profile is in the same position as when seen from the front.

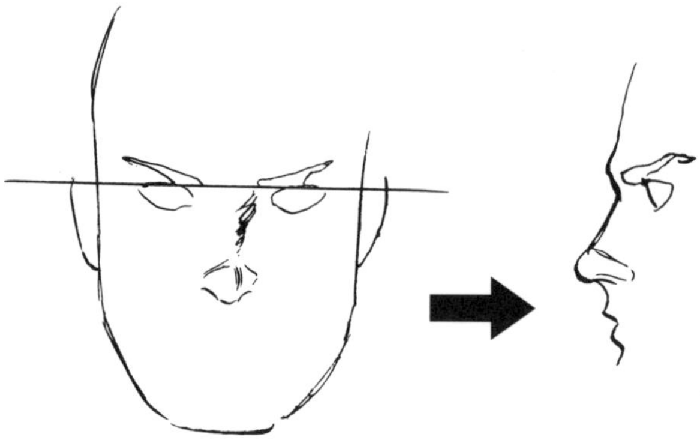

●The position of nose●

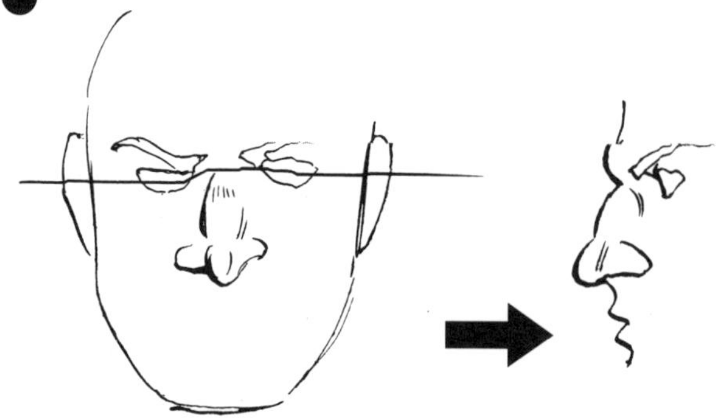

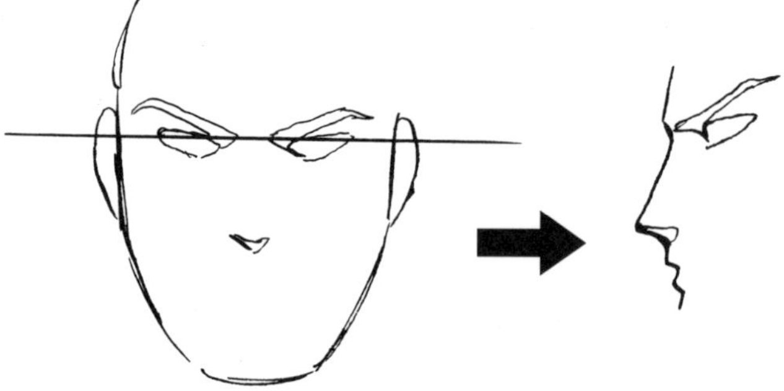

■FACE■

NOSE

●The variation of noses●

Although there are many ways to draw, I want you to aim for your original while referring to my examples.

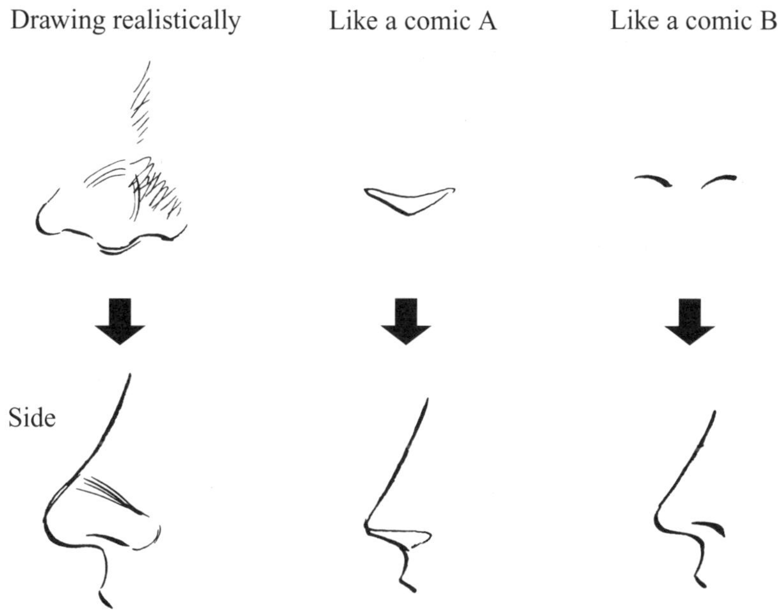

●The bridge of the nose
The bridge of the nose is difficult in line drawing. Although a profile is easy, it is not easy to express the bridge of the nose seen from the front. I want you to practice and research.

Expression of a hero's straight bridge of the nose is difficult.

A Expression using lines

B Expression using the line of the same curve

C Expression using a slash

It is easy to draw a villain's nose.

MOUTH

How the mouth is drawn plays a big role in the characterization of a character. The character will become cool or jocular depending on how you draw the mouth.

●The position of mouth●

The space between the mouth and nose is narrow.

Mouth is in an ordinary position.

Space between mouth and nose is wide.

●The variation of mouths●

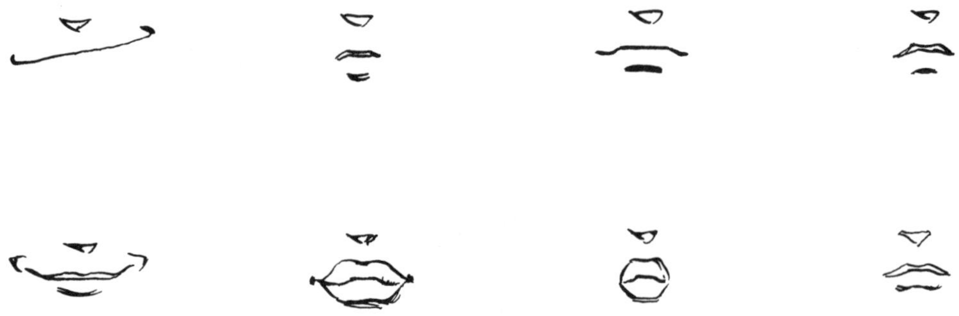

■FACE■

THE SHAPE OF FACE

●The shape of face●

Keeping the same nose and eyes, look at the difference by changing the shape of the face only.

Triangle

Normal

Square

●The variation of faces●

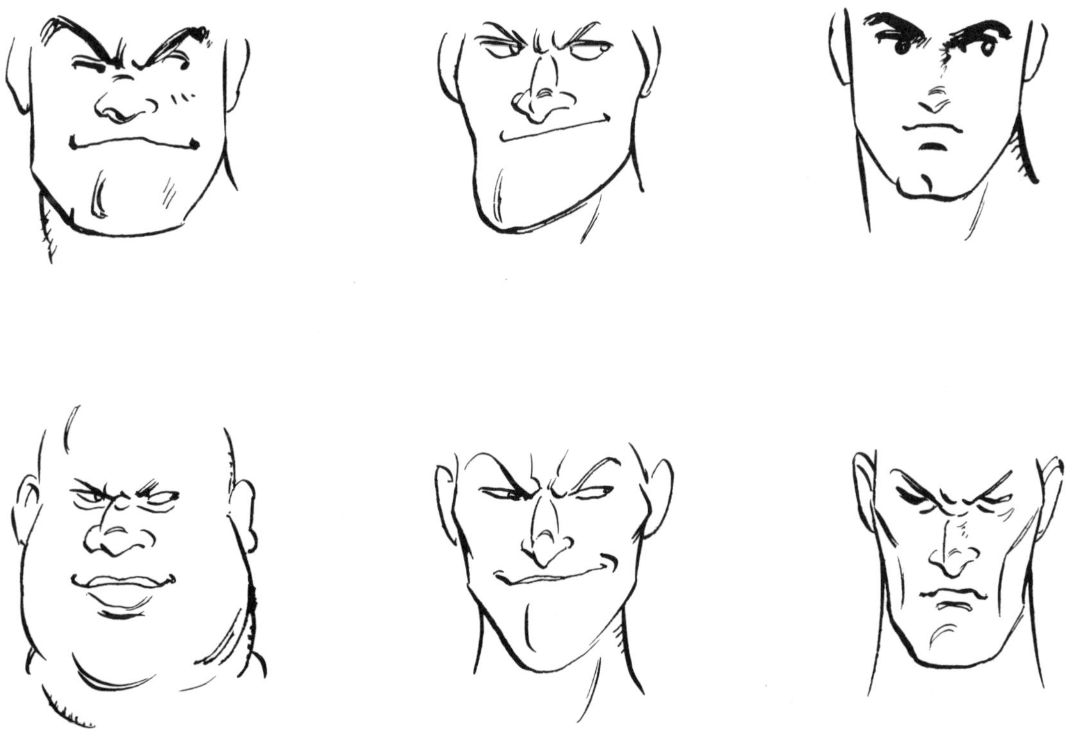

■FACE■

ANGLE

Let's study the face seen from various angles using an egg. As shown in a right figure, a line is drawn on the surface of an egg, an eye, a nose, and a mouth are drawn. Study the changes in the face from above, the sides and slanted.

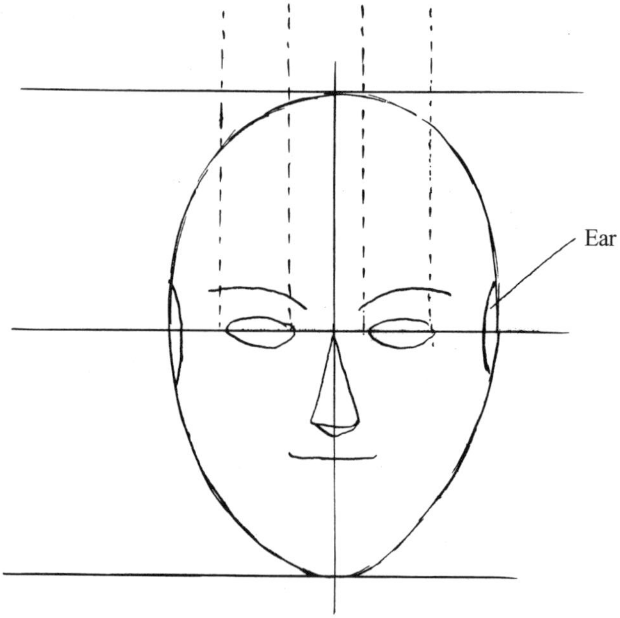

View from above

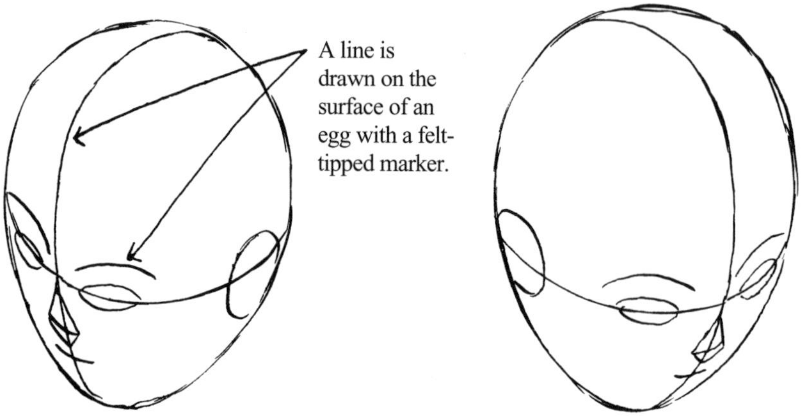

View from below

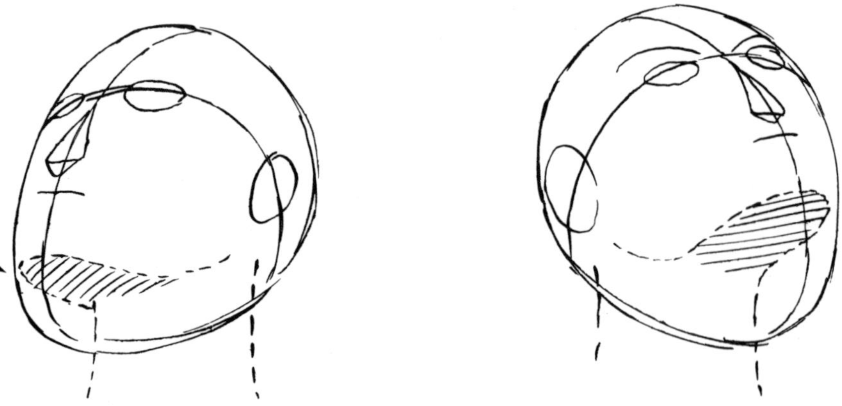

ANGLE

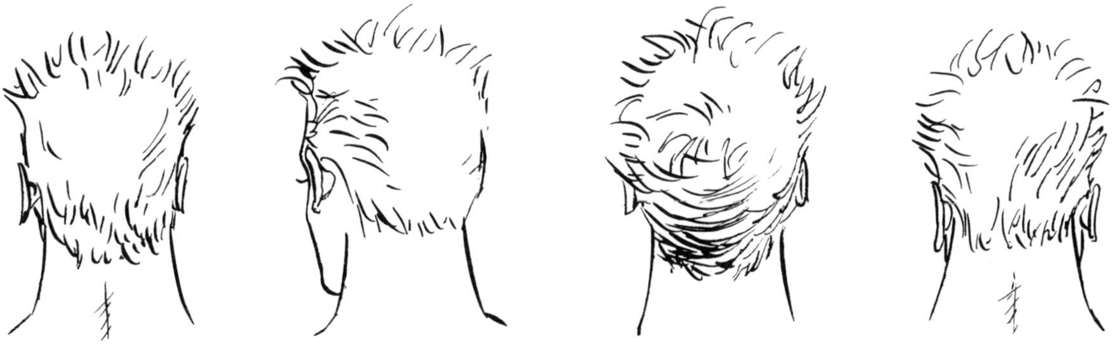

A face becomes long when the mouth is opened widely.

Mouth is closed. .

■FACE■

HAIR STYLE

Although drawing hair is an important element for drawing a face, there are few books that provide exact explanations. It is important not to over draw the lines.

●Arrange hair lines●

Long hair which is often seen in animation and comics.

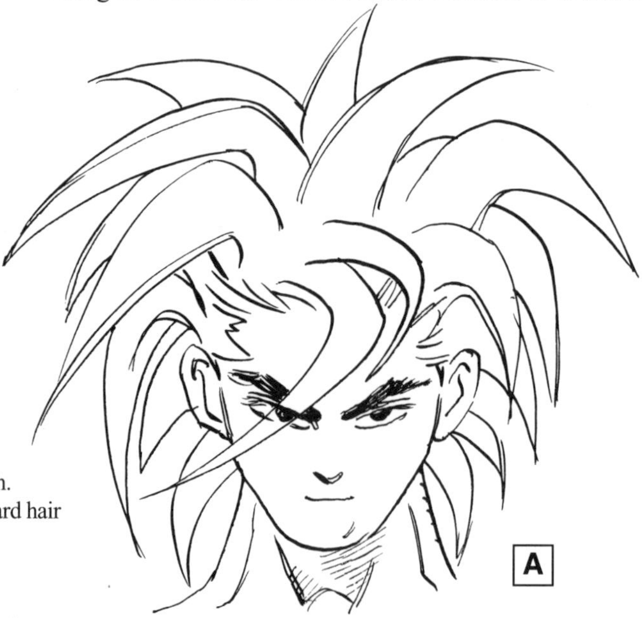

Draw a bunch.
Linear and hard hair

A

B

Hair soft with a curve

C

There are too many lines.
It will be better when it is shown in a bundle like A or B.

Super Character's

CHARACTERIZATION

■CHARACTERIZATION■

SMALL BUT STRONG

A powerful character can be made even if it is small. It is important to clearly think about the characters role. Furthermore, you can give the character individualy through the costumes etc.

An ordinary size

A Force is shown from his physique. He is a typical gangster type. His power is quite obvious. This is a so called typical character.

The character is powerful even if it is small.

B Although he has a small body, he has the power to hide some strange capability.

■CHARACTERIZATION■

POWER INSIDE

When creating a special character, it is not necessary to give it a build like a prowrestler.

B This is the same kind of uncanny character as A.

A There is also this kind of character who transmits an eeriness.

■CHARACTERIZATION■

DIFFERENT MEN

COSTUME

Naked, a thick belt, a sword on his back. Although he isn't wearing much it is still very powerful.

Costume is another important element to discribe the characters power.

It's a fancy costume like a super hero. It shows his hardness with a mysterious feeling.

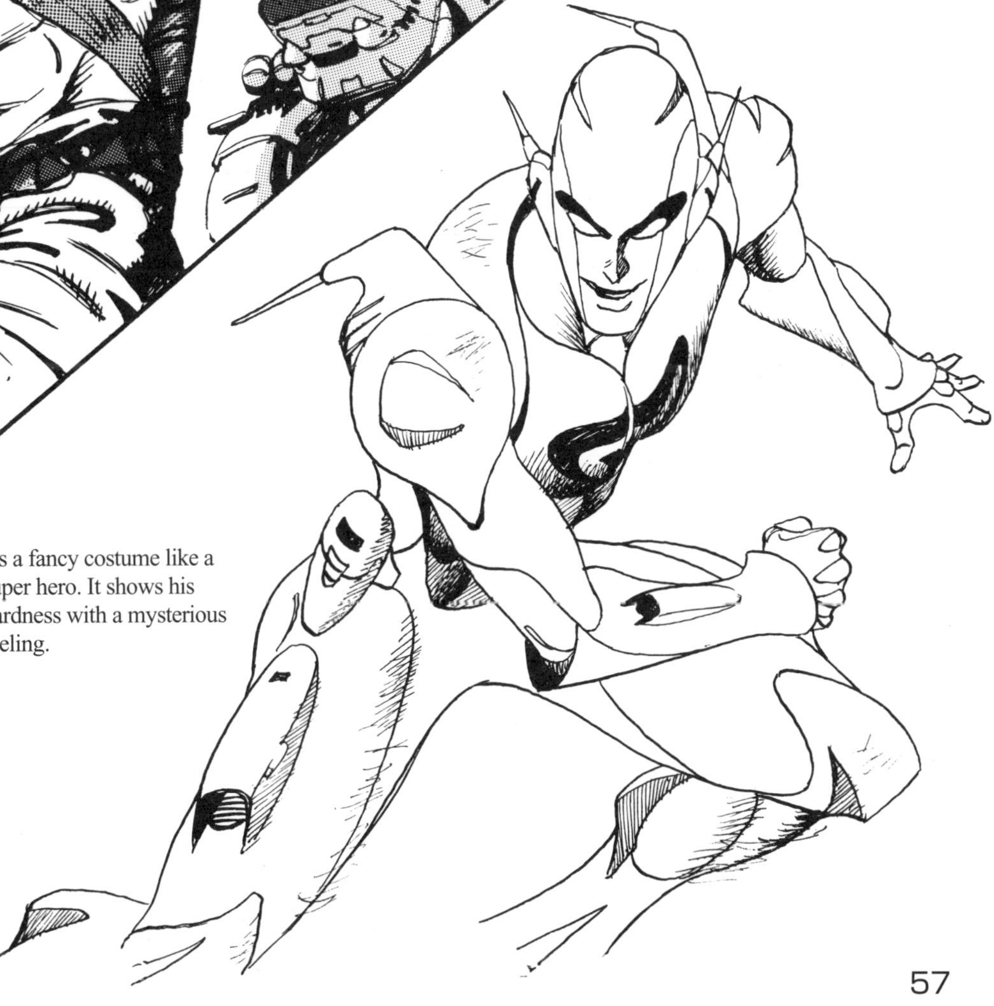

■CHARACTERIZATION■

COSTUME

Clothes can express the background of the character.

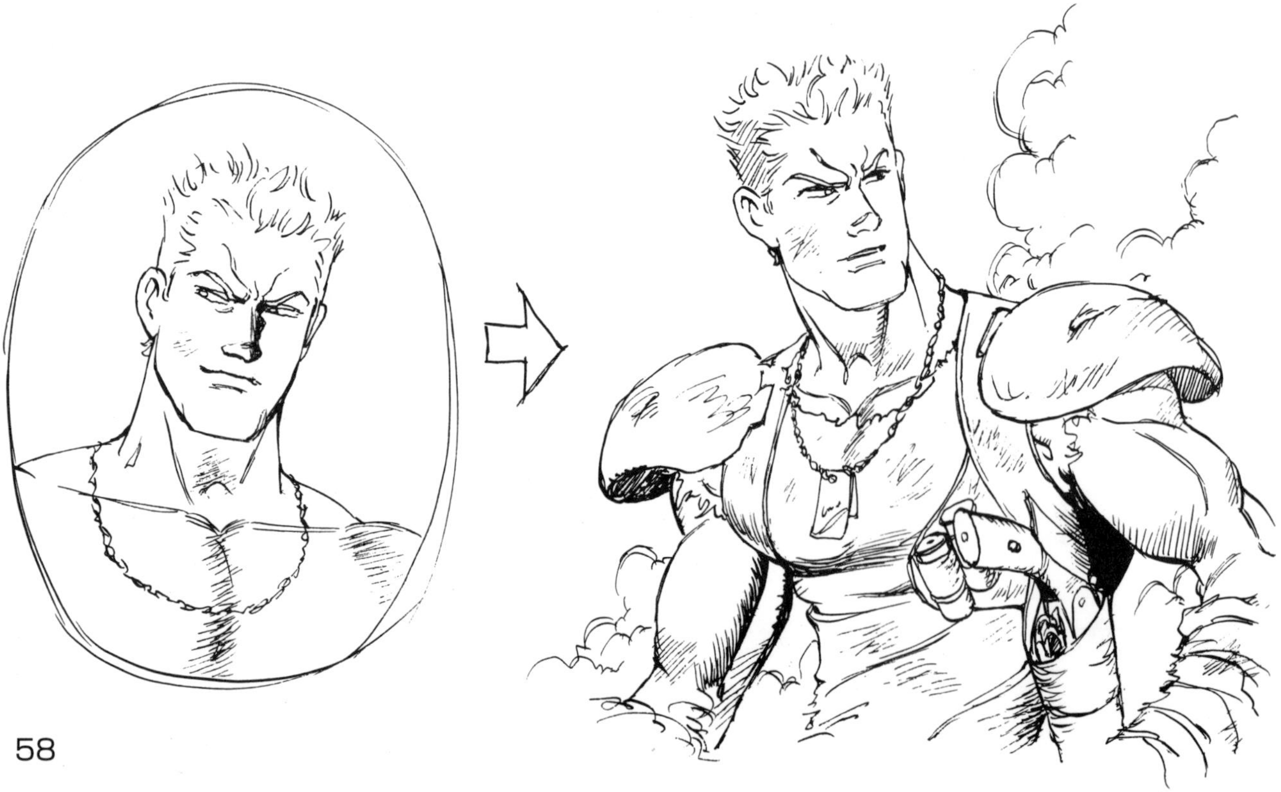

■CHARACTERIZATION■

UNEXPECTED NATURE

1 one The middle age man who is a good person. If he is evil.

2 two Actually he is a man with an evil spirit

If dress and a hairstyle are changed, force will come out further.

1 one He seems like a weak boy but suppose he is the leader of a gang.

He looks sly!

2 two An uncanny image like a pervert.

You should know many genres.

It is extremely helpful to have knowledge of various genres when you are drawing pictures or creating a story for a comic. I acquired my information from foreign films. When I was in 6th grade at elementary school I saw my first film which starred Vivien Leigh. Although this was a movie for grownups, I was fascinated by its romantic story (I had become precocious.). I studied characterization, creating a feeling for scenes from various genres including, of course action, Japanese sword fighting, Yuujiro Ishihara films and SF etc. Therefore I believe these films have greatly helped me to create scenes.

Super Character's

PEN&TECHNIQUE

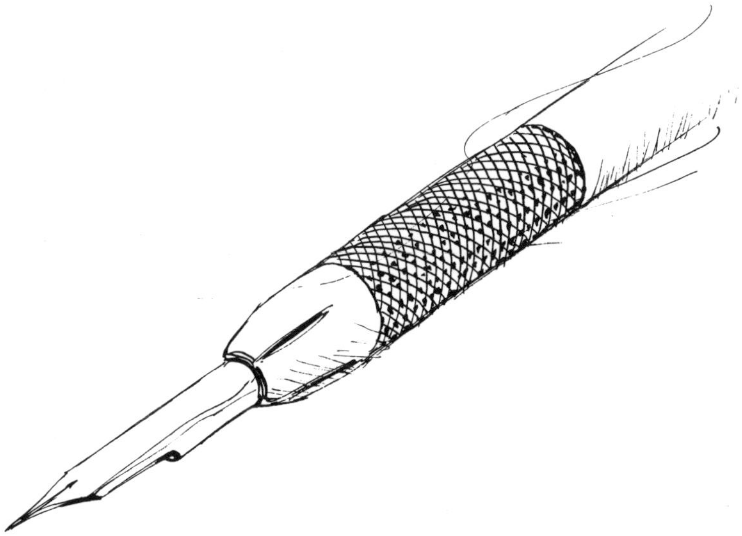

■PEN&TECHNIQUE■

PEN

I mainly use a circle pen for drafting. The circle pen is hard and can draw very thin lines and very thick lines. If you sharpen it on a whetstone, it draws line new again. It is practical and economical pen.

●The variation of pens●

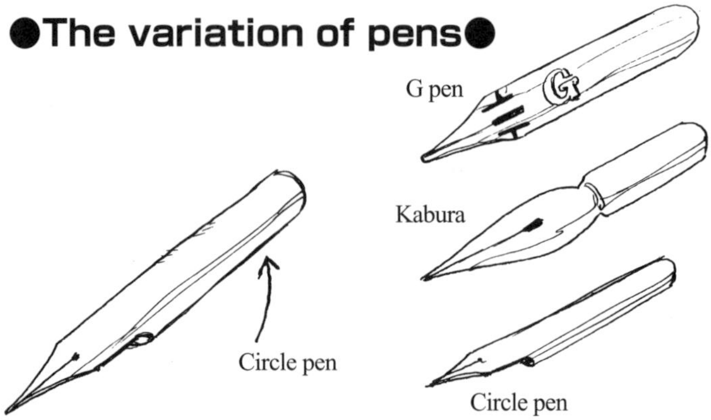

Oblique lines by circle pen

●The line drawn with the circle pen

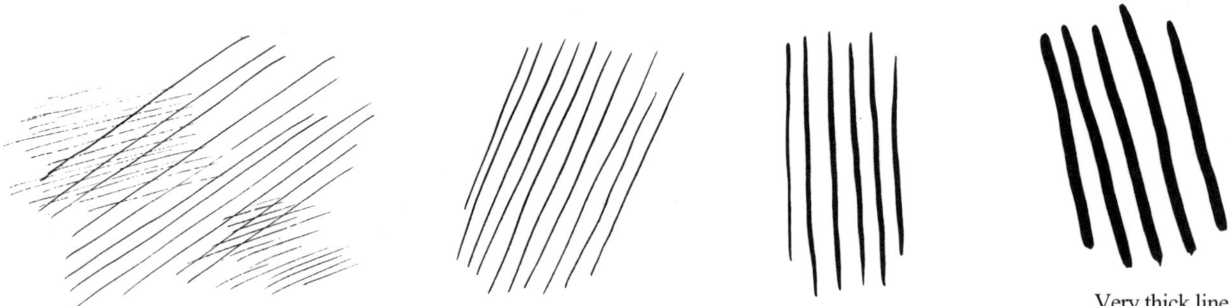
Thin line

Comparatively thin line

Thick line

Very thick line

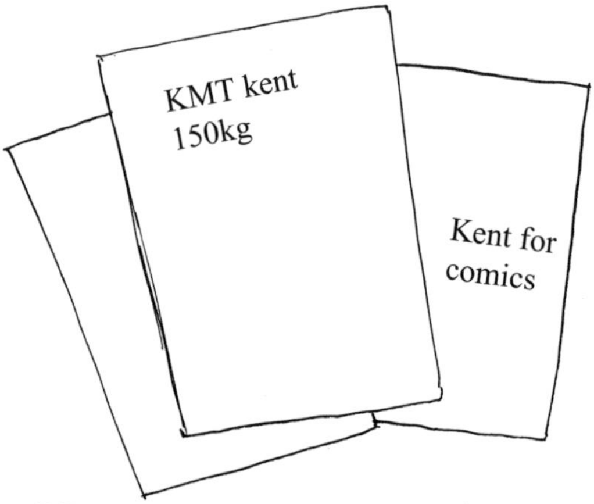

●Paper

It is important to choose the right paper so that the pen doesn't catch on the paper. Test various types and choose the one that suits you. I use 150kg KMK Kent.

●Ink

Water resistant ink is better because it does not melt and run when using white correction fluid. I use black from Holbein waterproof color inks.

PEN

In order to master the circle pen you will need to practice. Compared to other pens it is quite strong. However, once you get used to it, it is an exellent pen and you won't be able to part with it.

●The variation of expression by circle pen●

A An illustration drawn with a thin line

B An illustration combining thin and thick lines

C An illustration drawn with only thick line

■PEN&TECHNIQUE■

OBLIQUE STROKES

Use the oblique strokes mainly to achieve a cubic effect and the feeling of quality.

Softness changes by the angle of oblique strokes.

A

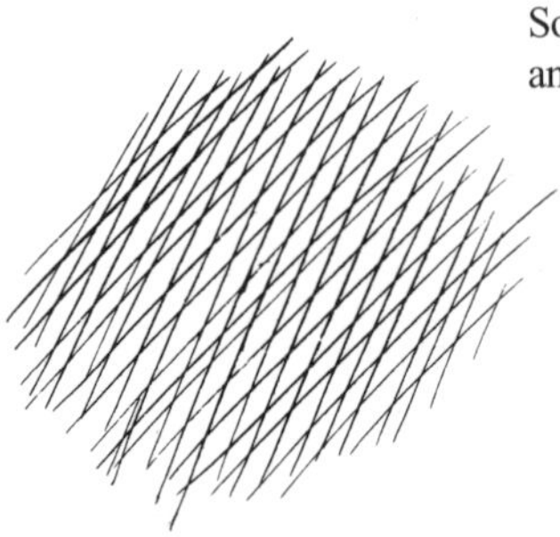

Hold a pen lightly and draw softly.

B

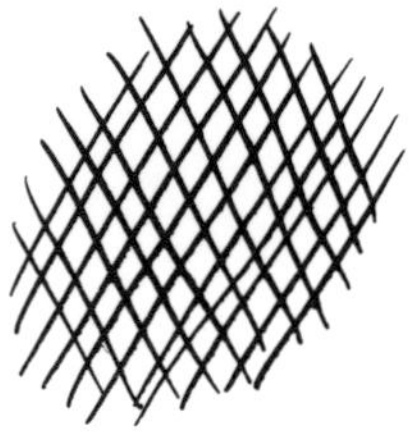

B is almost ineffective except for special usage.

■Texture example■

The flow of a slash is arranged when drawing a griddle.

Dustcloth

Jeans

Many things were expressed by using touches in practice A. Establish your own expression.

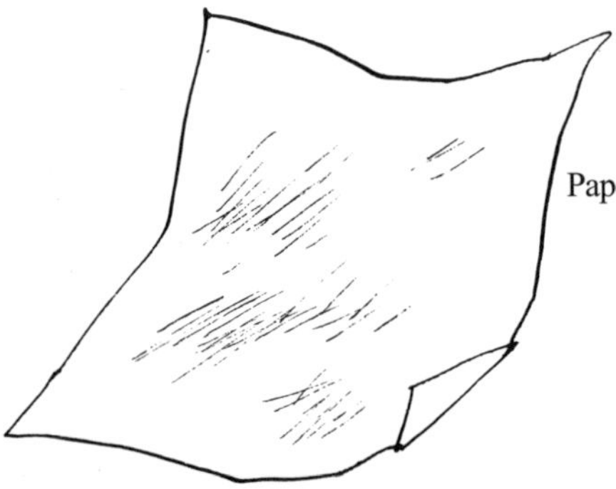

Paper

Let's draw oblique lines well without crossing them.

■PEN&TECHNIQUE■

SOLIDITY

A This is often used in American comics.

B By one thin line

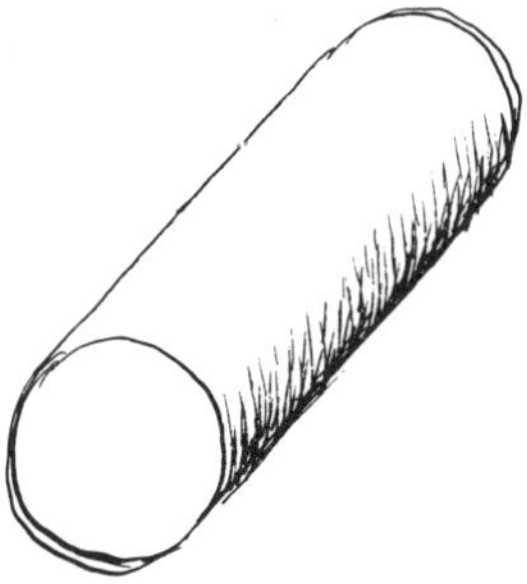

C It is drawn by crossing lines. You can see that the thinner the lines the more realistic it becomes.

■Texture example■

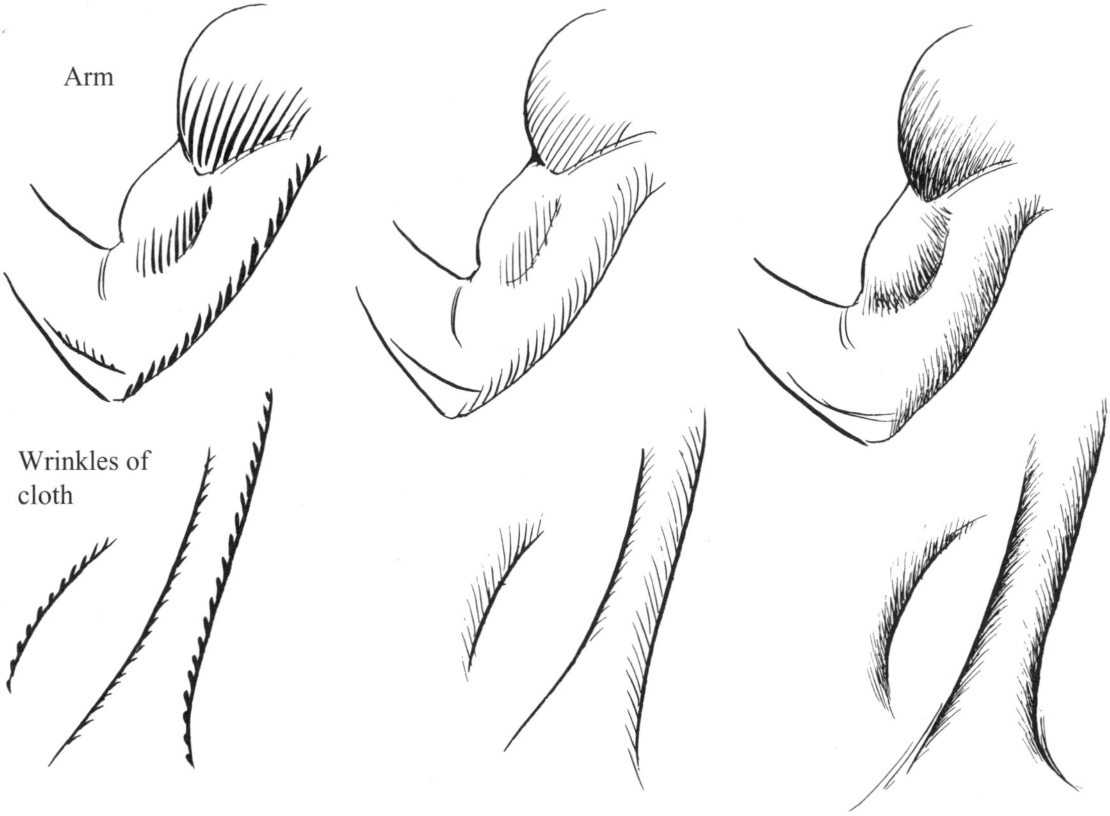

■PEN&TECHNIQUE■

ONE POINT ADVICE

1 one Buy one Figure super hero! If you have Superman or Batman, practice drawing a body by referring to this figure.

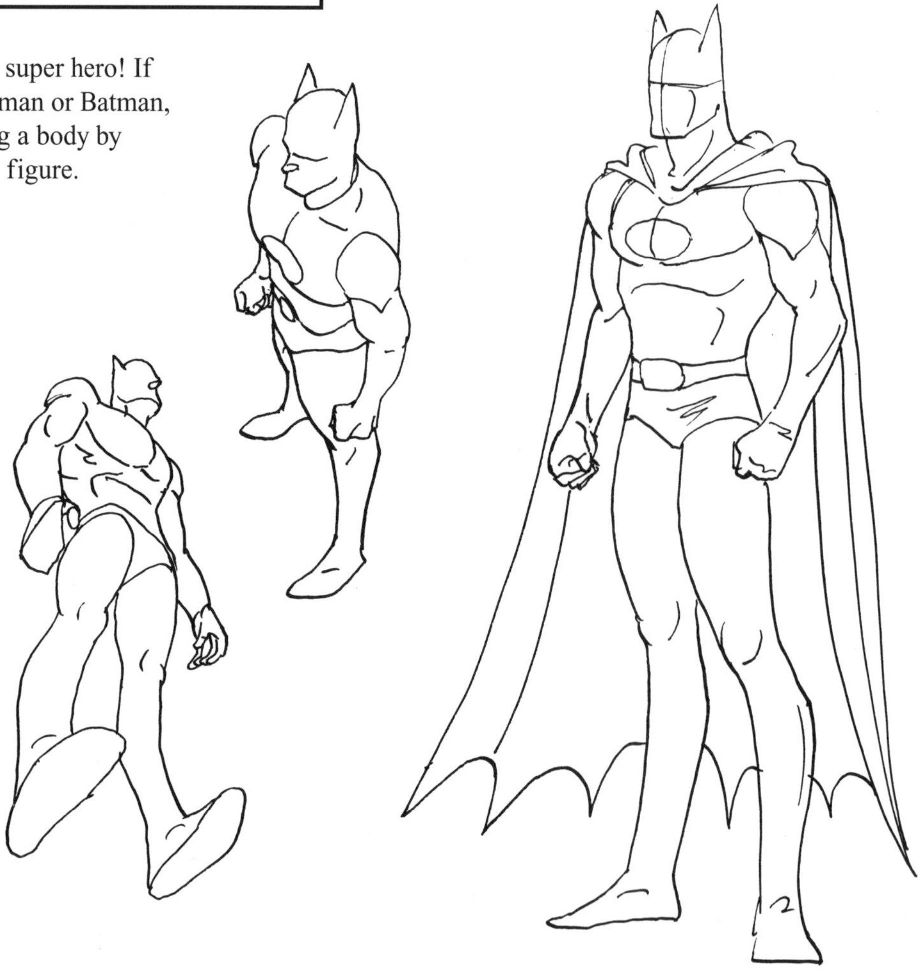

2 two Refer to reference material. When drawing bodies refer to prowrestling or combative sports magazines. When drawing mechanics refer to a motercycle or a car magazines.

3 three Use a mirror! It is very convenient if you always prepare a mirror on your desk. It is useful especially when drawing a hand. You can draw a hand holding a glass etc, while looking at it in the mirror.

4 four You can make a character more powerful by exaggerating one portion of the same pose.

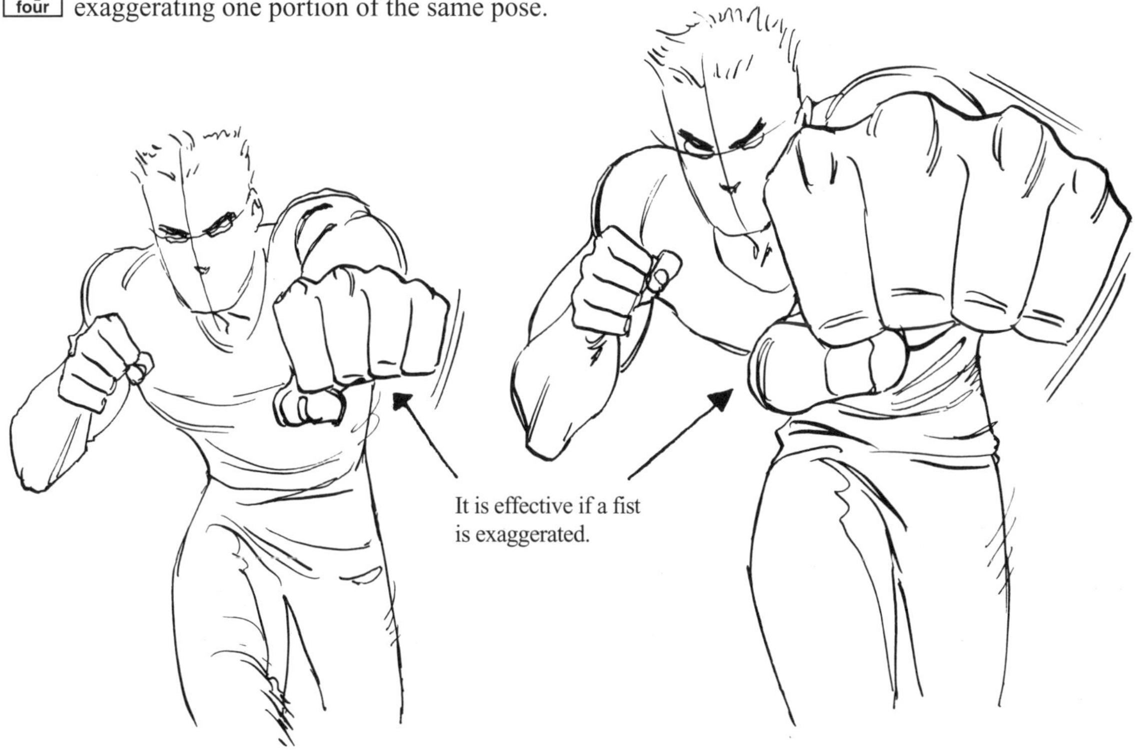

■PEN&TECHNIQUE■

ZOOM

The more exaggerated, the more effective. I compared the lower figures.

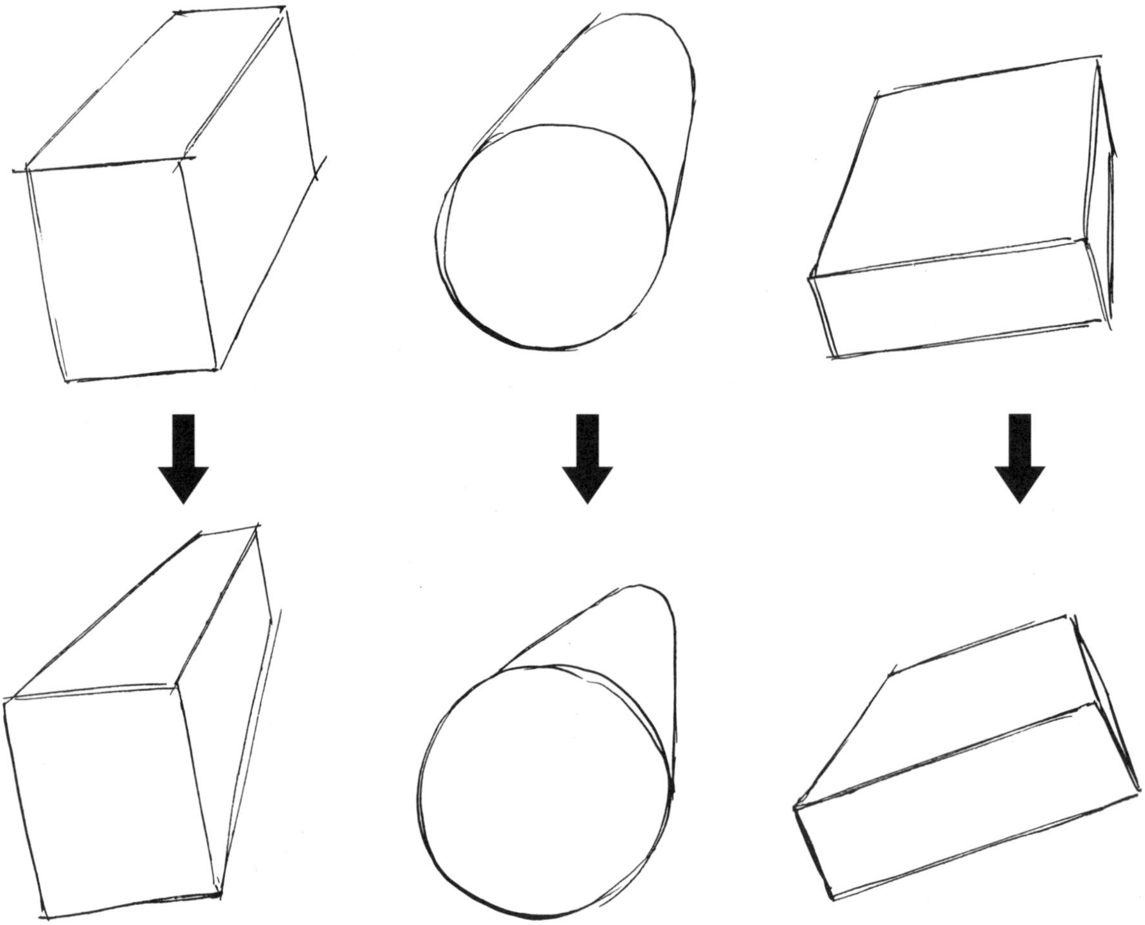

As shown in the left example, force changes by how it is exaggerated. If it is actually used in an illustration or a comic it will turn out like the left example.

Super Character's

POSES

NUDE

NUDE

※I enlarged this leg to show force and a sense of stability.

NUDE

The right leg is enlarged to show the distance from the left leg.

In order to emphasize force, draw bigger.
In order to emphasize force, draw bigger.

NUDE

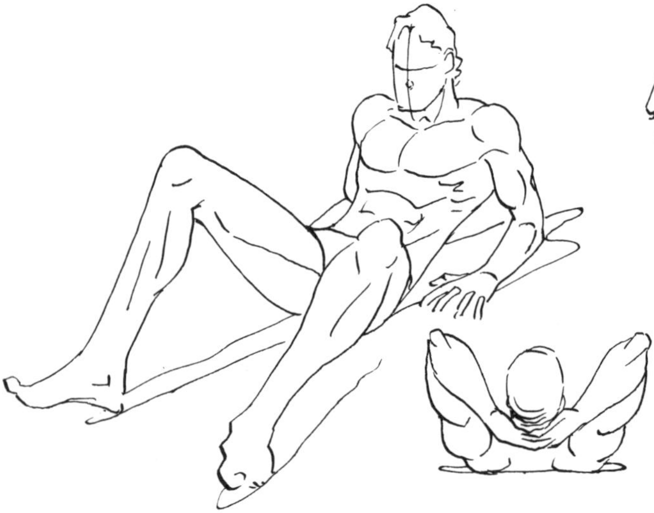

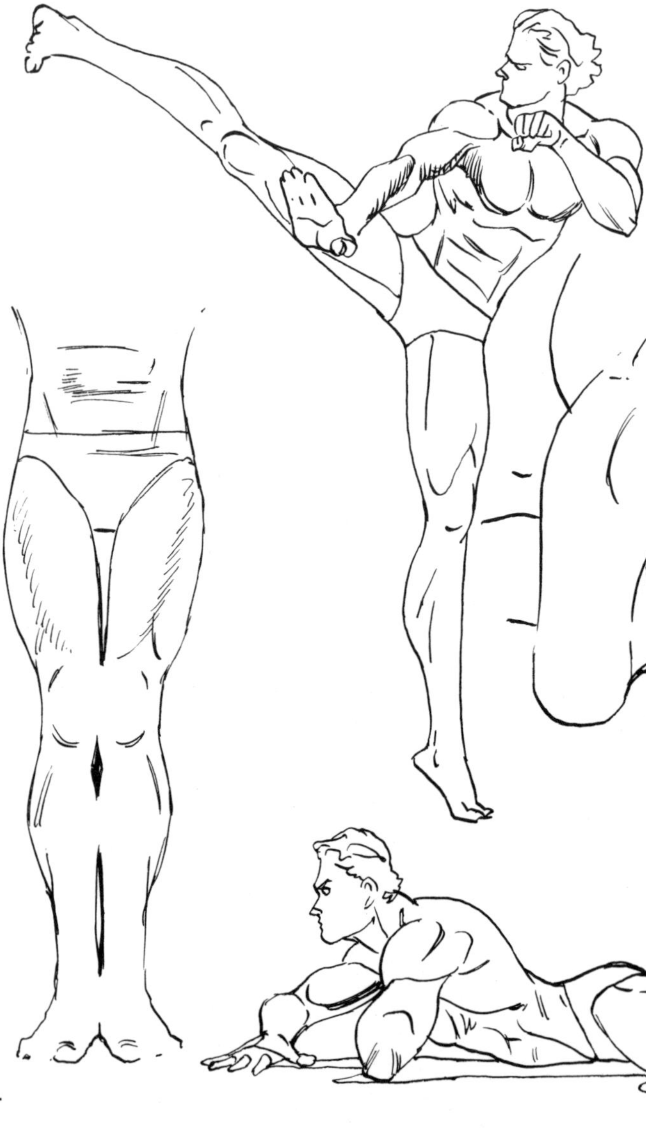

FLY

WHAOOO

BLADE

BLADE

RUN

RUN

STEP

STEP

KICK

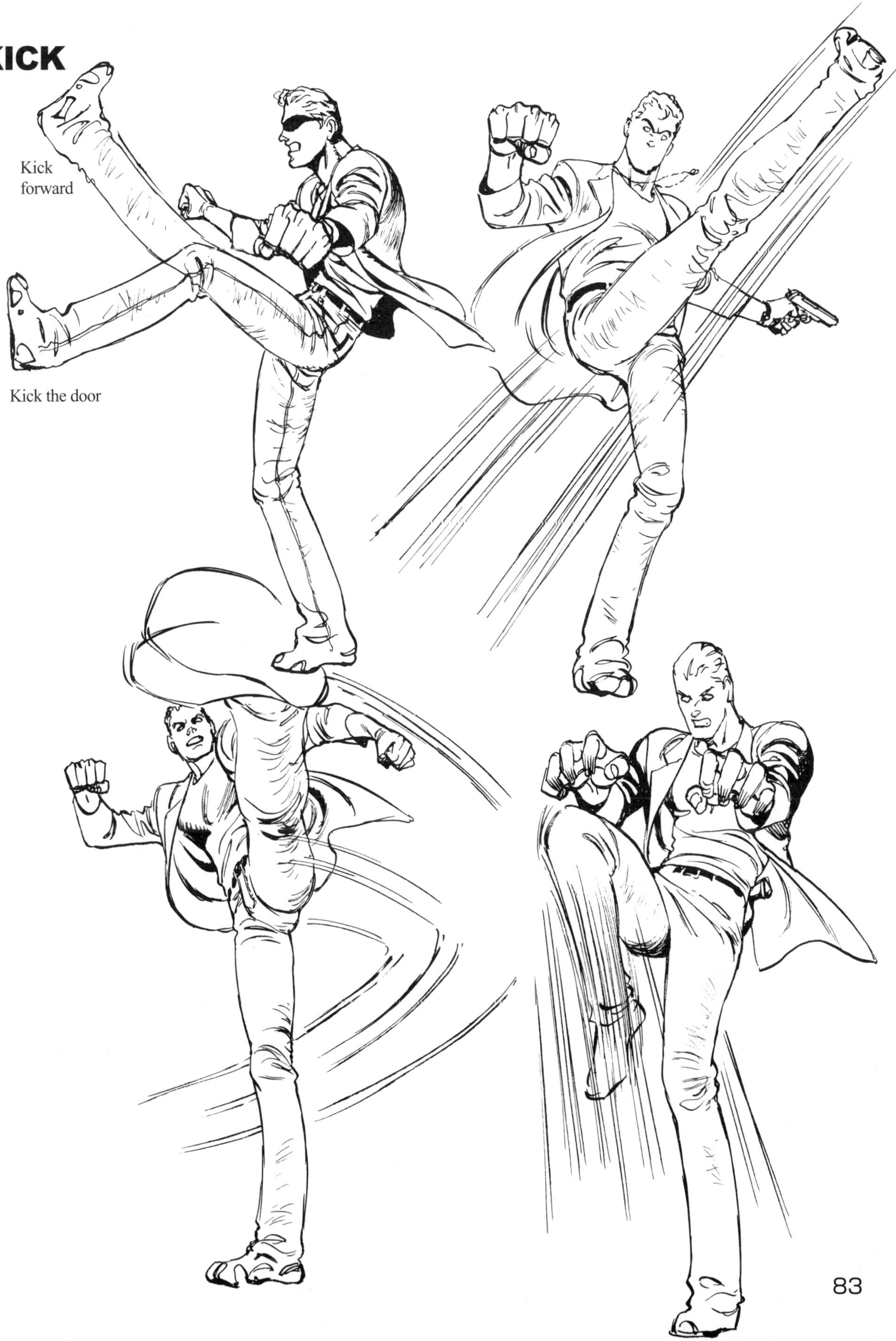

Kick forward

Kick the door

KICK

KICK

PUNCH

PUNCH

PUNCH

PUNCH

PUNCH

SHOT

SHOT

ド
ガ

SHOT

SHOT

SHOT RIFLE

SHOT RIFLE

SHOTGUN

HiYUN
BUN

THROW

DON

LIFT

THROW

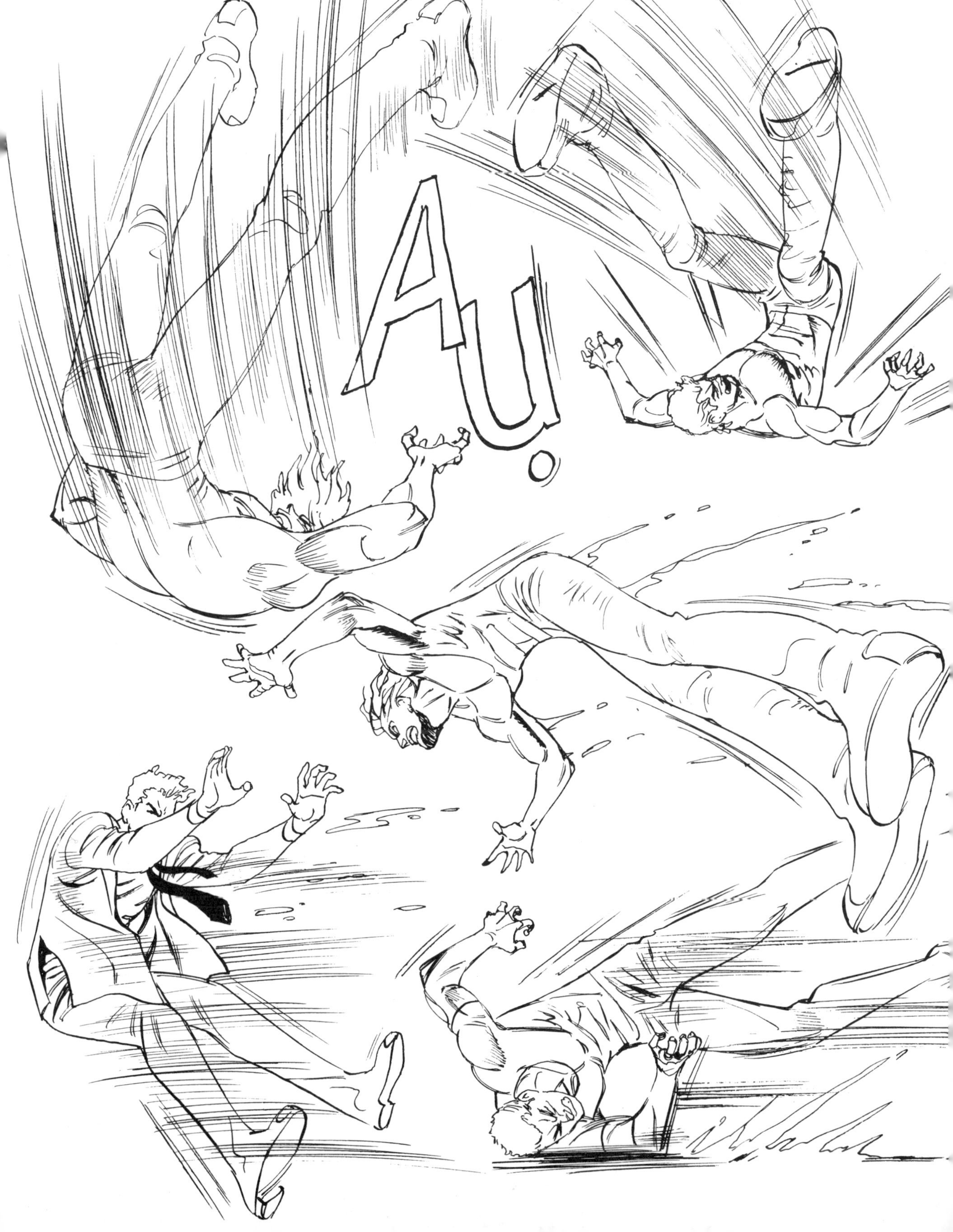

BICYCLE

BODY ATTACK

Mu.

LADDER

DRAW A GUN

COOL POSE

COOL POSE

SIT

HAND

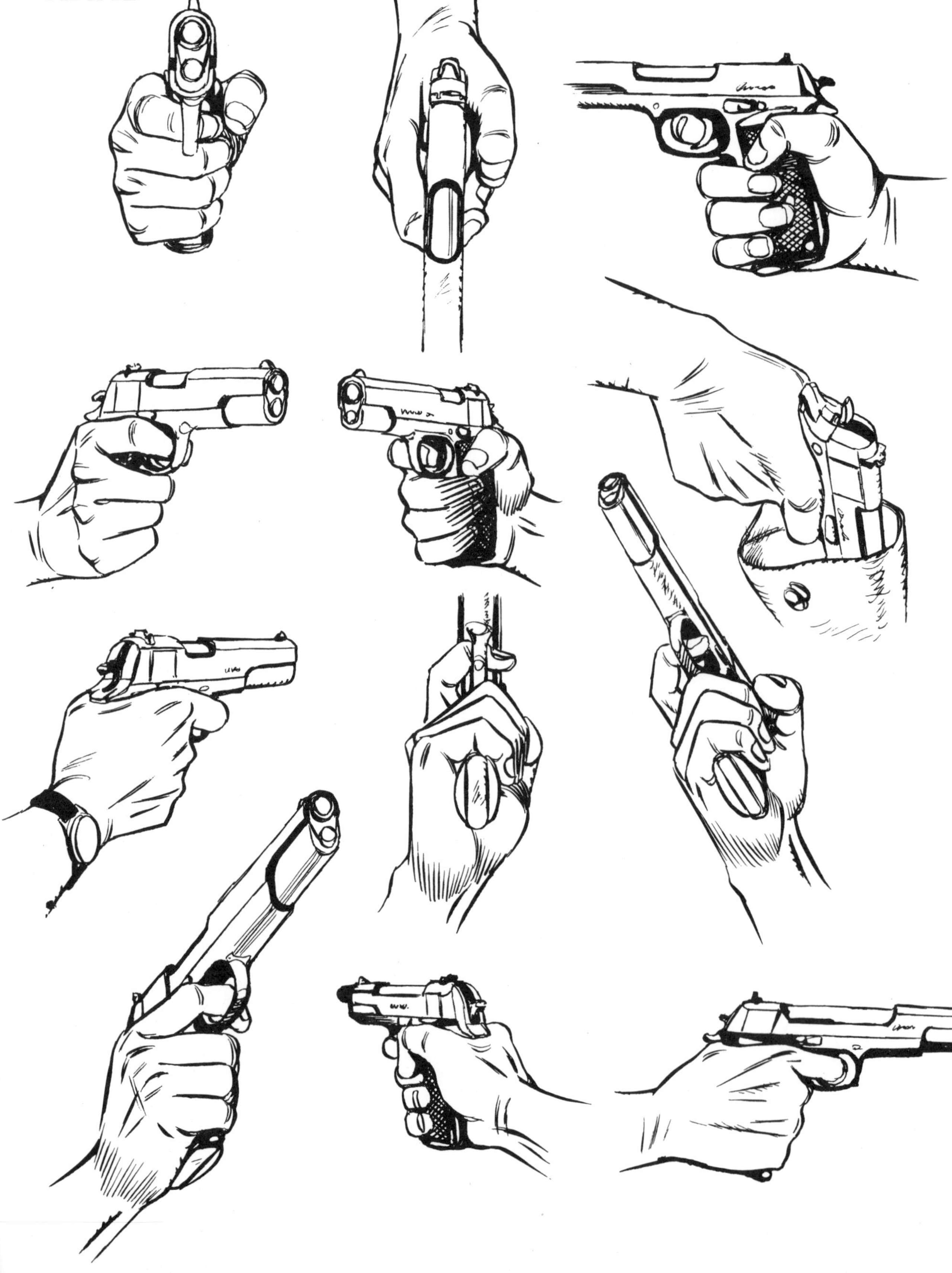

HAND

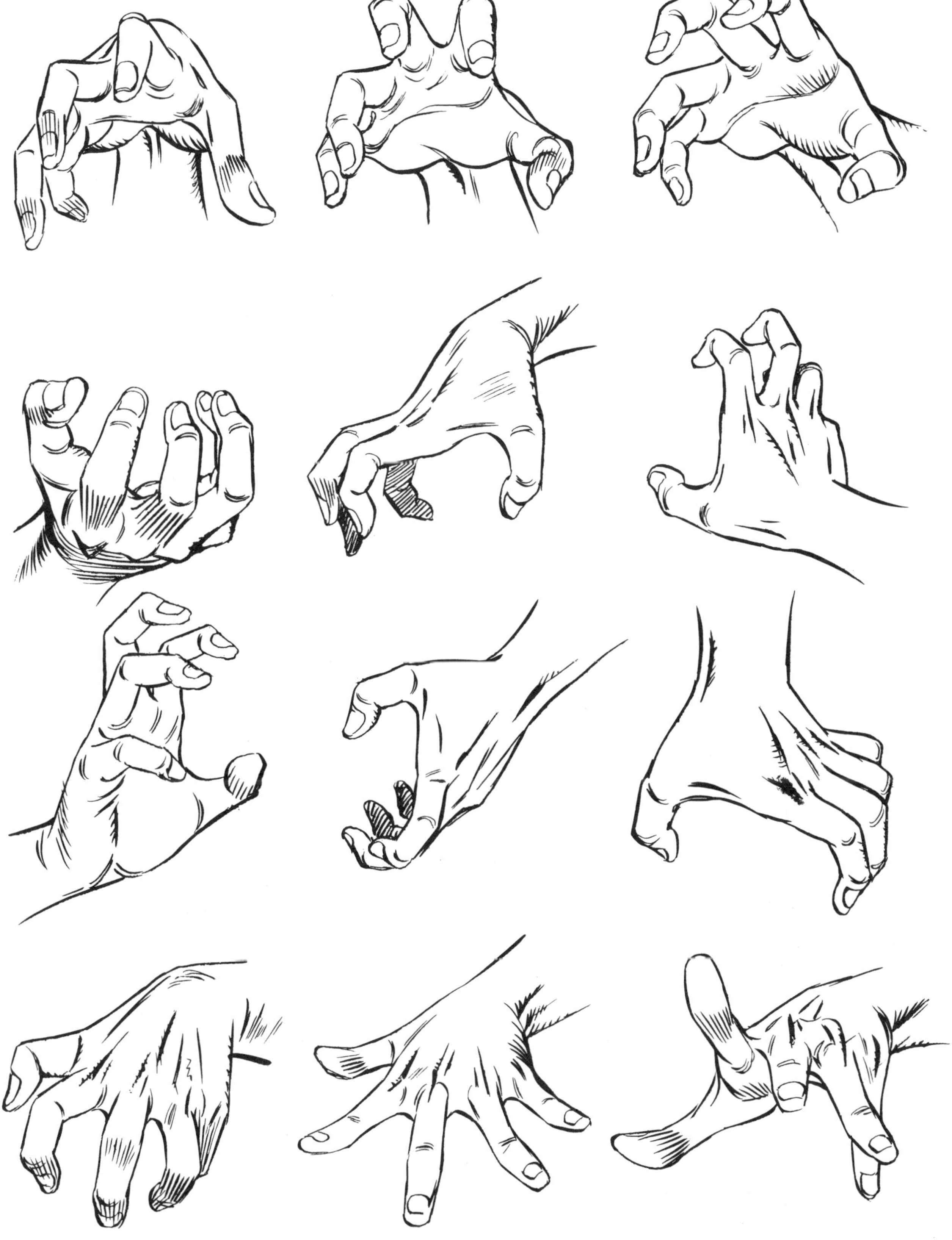

HAND

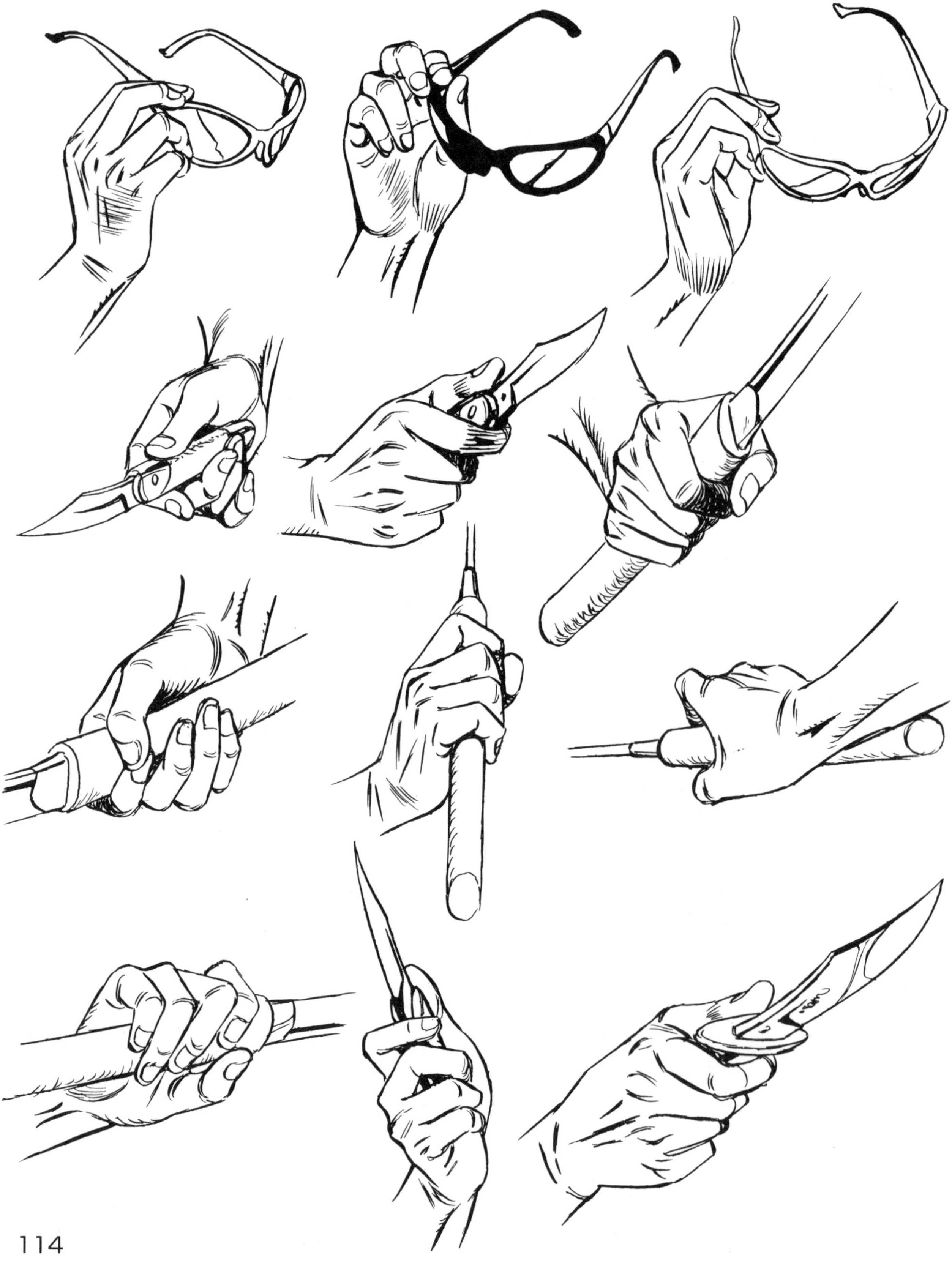

HAND

HAND

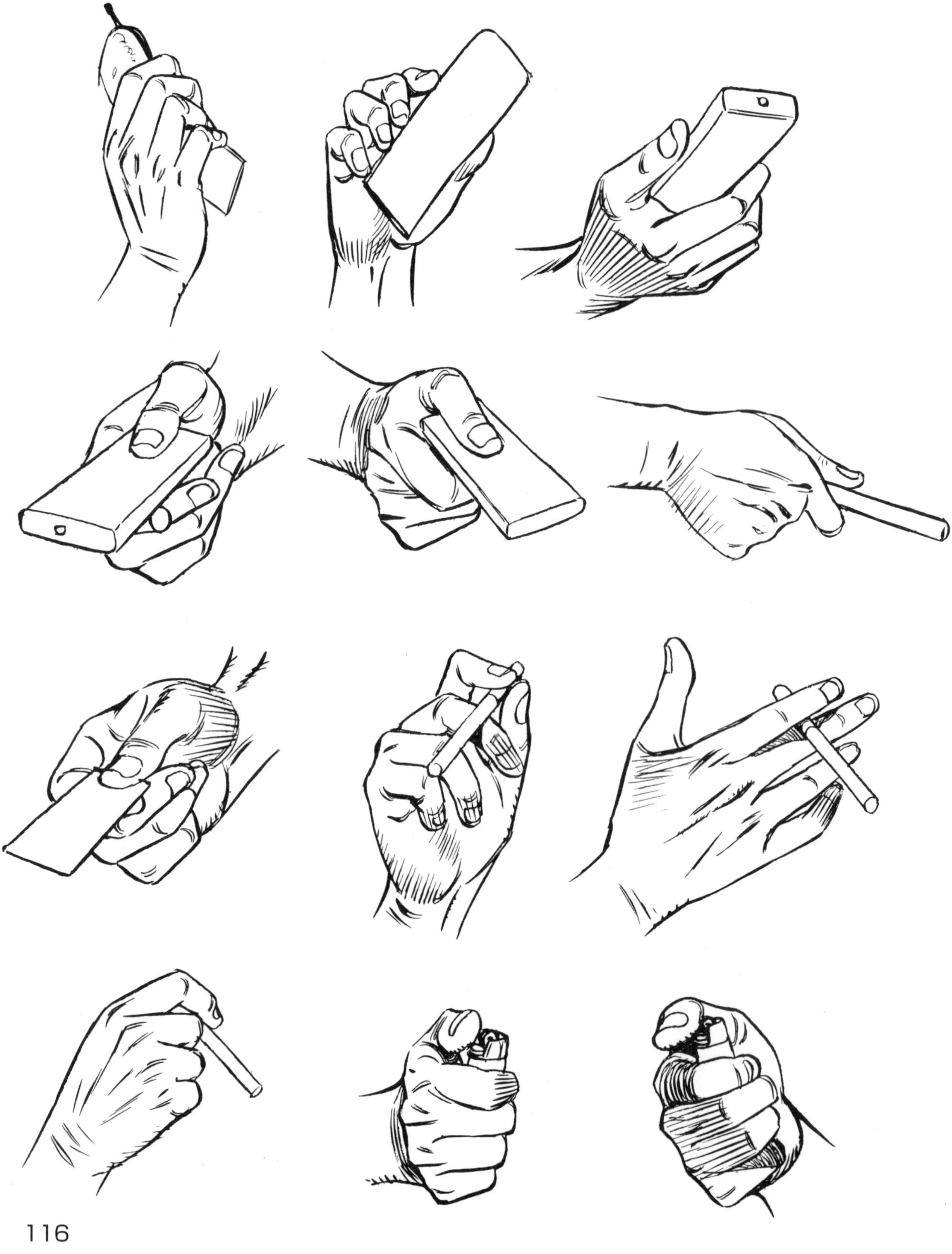

SUITS

SUITS

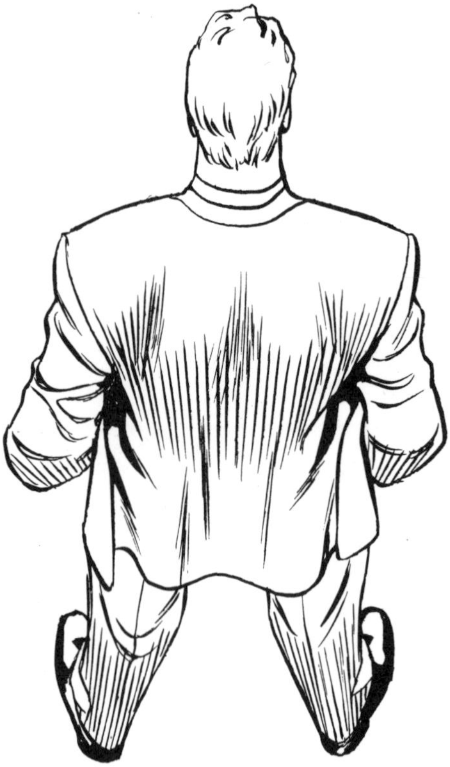

SUITS

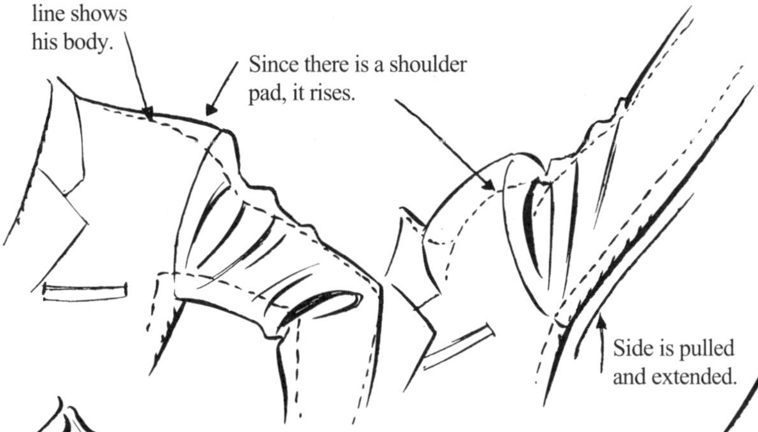

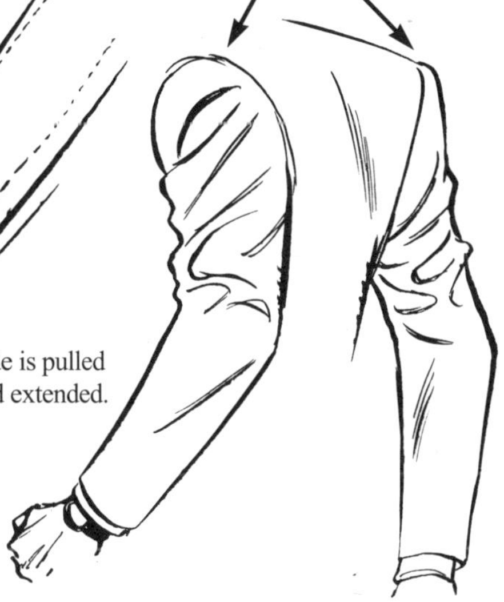

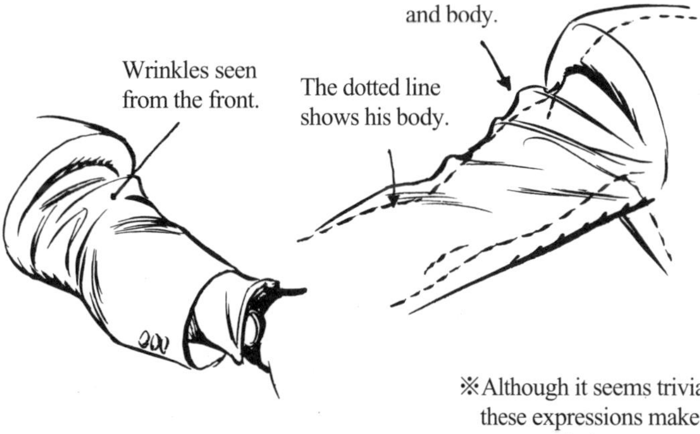

※Although it seems trivial, these expressions make it more realistic.

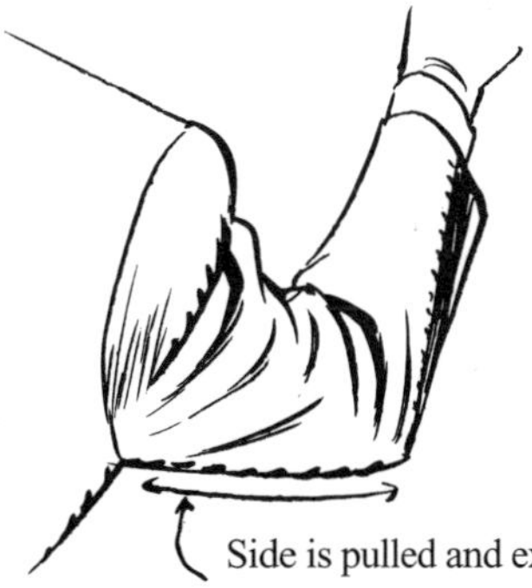